The

Moon
Gardener's
Almanac
2018

Created by Céleste
Edited by Thérèse Trédoulat
Translated by Mado Spiegler

First published in French as *Jardinez avec la Lune 2018*
by Éditions Rustica in 2017
This edition published in English by Floris Books in 2017
© 2017 Éditions Rustica, Paris
English version © 2017 Floris Books

MIX
Paper from
responsible sources
FSC® C007785

British Library CIP data available
ISBN 978-178250-425-2
Printed in Great Britain by
Bell & Bain, Ltd

The
Moon
Gardener's
Almanac
2018

Floris
Books

Contents

Foreword

This calendar shows you the best times for sowing, grafting and harvesting aerial parts of plants, and planting, dividing, pruning and harvesting roots during the different phases of the Moon.

Based on 35 years' experience of gardening by the Moon, this calendar will help you to garden successfully from January 1 to December 31 using the lunar cycle as your guide. As a result, your garden and harvest will be all the more beautiful and abundant. Day by day, the calendar suggests favourable times for working with leaves, flowers, fruit or roots. But it also discusses less favourable times for gardening – apogees, perigees, lunar nodes, eclipses – which you can use to your best advantage, or just take a well-deserved rest.

You can also use the calendar to make notes about the weather, temperature and air pressure (pp. 88–103). These factors are highly influential for effective gardening, and by comparing several years in a row, you can follow the evolution of the climate and adapt your gardening methods accordingly.

If the weather is unfavourable on a particular day, or it's not convenient to perform the task specified in the calendar, take a look at the crop tables, which offer alternative dates for sowing, planting and pruning according to the Moon.

We wish you happy reading, and fruitful gardening!

The Moon
and the
Garden

Rhythms of the Earth

The life rhythms of our Earth involve three recurring processes: the annual cycle ruled by the Sun; the monthly cycle ruled by the Moon; and the daily cycle, ruled by the alternation of day and night.

Annual cycle

To help us understand the path of the Moon and its effects, which are the foundation of our gardening calendar, let's first look at the path of the Sun in the temperate zone of the Northern hemisphere.

Winter and spring

On the winter solstice, December 21 (the shortest day of the year, varying in the UK from 8 hours 3 minutes in Penzance, Cornwall, to only 5 hours 49 minutes in Lerwick, Shetland), the Sun rises well to the south-east and makes its lowest arc of the year, setting far in the south-west. By this time, many plants have died or are lying dormant in the soil. The Earth begins to prepare for its renewal – the new solar year is starting.

From the shortest day onwards to the summer solstice on June 21 (the longest day of the year, varying from 16 hours 23 minutes in Penzance to 18 hours 55 minutes in Lerwick), the Sun rises higher and higher in the sky. It ascends from Sagittarius, the lowest constellation, to Taurus and Gemini, the highest constellations. During these six months, very gradually, the Earth warms up. As the midday Sun gets higher in the sky and the days get longer, sap becomes active in the plant world.

It is then that we witness a veritable resurrection of nature, which guides the gardener's many tasks: pruning fruit and ornamental trees, soil preparation, sowing and replanting. In June, this time of intense growth comes to an end, as does summer sowing – harvesting is about to start.

Summer and autumn

On June 21, the day of the summer solstice, the Sun starts its descending arc. Its warm rays now have a drying effect. The days grow shorter, crops are harvested and the Earth starts to become bare. The rise of sap also slows down, causing tree leaves to dry out.

After the autumn equinox on September 22, gardeners can gradually start to work the soil in preparation for the following year.

With every harvest, the soil becomes less fertile, its vital resources exhausted by the crops, vegetables and fruit it has nourished. We need to help it restore itself by providing refined compost, enlivening manures and invigorating green manures.

During this period of deep inhalation, the Earth absorbs all the fertilising and rebalancing elements that gardeners provide. Sap descends into the roots again, leaves blow away, days get shorter and shorter and winter arrives. At the lowest point of the cycle, with the Sun back in Sagittarius, a new exhalation is about to begin.

Now, on warm, calm days, is the time for gardeners to plant perennials, trees and bare-root bushes.

Position of the Earth in relation to the constellations of the zodiac

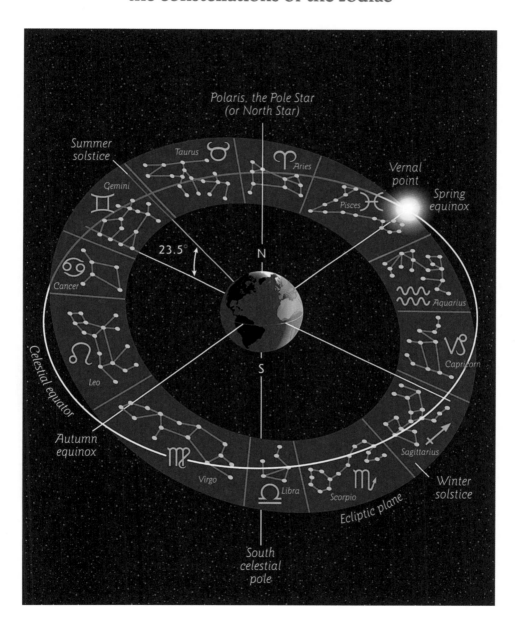

Polaris, the Pole Star
(or North Star)

Summer
solstice

Taurus

Aries

Gemini

Vernal
point

Spring
equinox

Pisces

23.5°

N

Aquarius

Cancer

S

Capricorn

Leo

Celestial equator

Autumn
equinox

Virgo

Libra

Scorpio

Sagittarius

Winter
solstice

Ecliptic plane

South
celestial
pole

Monthly cycle

The Moon takes one lunar month to orbit the Earth (approximately 27 days). Just as the Sun does in one year, in one month the Moon passes in front of every zodiacal constellation, with profound effects upon the Earth. The most spectacular example of this is illustrated by the phenomenon of the tides, which follow the rhythm of the 'Moon Day' of 24 hours and 50 minutes, of the Moon's rising, culminating, setting, reaching its lowest point and rising again. Scientific experiments have shown that the effect of the Moon can even be measured on inland water bodies.

Try looking up at the sky every evening. Whenever you can see the Moon, select landmarks (perhaps a tree, a house, or a hill) to locate it in relation to your environment. Day after day, you will observe the Moon ascending or descending in relation to these landmarks.

A number of online and print resources will give you daily times of the moonrise and moonset, which, on average, are about 50 minutes later every day.

Ascending moon: the lunar 'spring'

For 13 1/2 days, the Moon ascends from Sagittarius, the lowest constellation, to Taurus/Gemini, the highest. It follows the path taken by the Sun from December 21 to June 21.During this time, sap rises in all plant life, swelling their aerial parts. Now is the time to remove grafts for later use (making sure to keep them at the right temperature until it's time to graft them). It is also time for sowing seeds, harvesting leafy vegetables, juicy fruit, and cutting flowers for bouquets.

Descending moon: the lunar 'autumn'

For the next 13 1/2 days, as the Moon descends from Taurus to Sagittarius, it will appear lower and lower on the horizon every day. It follows the path taken by the Sun from June 21 to December 21. The sap goes back down into the roots and, as in October, the earth is at its most absorbent.

Using a tree as a landmark, look at the Moon and make a note of the time.
Look at it the next day, an hour later. If the Moon is higher, it is ascending; if it is lower, it is descending.

Now is the time to plant, replant, spread compost and organic manures, and prune. Plants recover better during this time: the roots reach deeper; the earth assimilates fertilizers well; hedges tolerate pruning without any problem, and the wounds left by removing tree branches heal better.

We call the ascending and descending movement of the Moon in a month (to be precise, 27 days, 7 hours, 43 minutes and 11 seconds) the sidereal period. **It is this ascending and descending motion that is relevant in the garden.**

Waxing and waning moon

Another cycle, called the synodic period (or synodic month) also takes approximately one month (to be precise, 29 days, 12 hours, 44 minutes and 3 seconds). **We do not take this cycle into account when gardening with the Moon.**

During the synodic month, the Moon waxes from New Moon to Full Moon, with the nearest side becoming increasingly visible. A thin sickle appears, which grows larger every day, to become the First Quarter and eventually the Full Moon.

The Moon then wanes to a New Moon. At the time of the Full Moon, it is fully illuminated by the Sun and looks completely round, waning daily until it disappears again at the time of the New Moon.

NOTE: Do not confuse the ascending moon with the waxing moon, or the descending moon with the waning moon.

Daily cycle

If you have ever camped in the woods, you will have been woken by a marvellous chorus of birdsong an hour or two before sunrise. The air grows colder, humidity rises, and plants also awaken, opening up to the morning dew and starting to swell with sap.

In the morning, when the dew has disappeared, it's time to sow seeds and pick lettuce, spinach, cucumbers and anything else that grows above ground.

Later, between midday and 3 pm, as the Sun starts to descend, the Earth turns back inward and forces move towards plants' roots. Now is the time to plant, replant, harvest root vegetables and finally, after sundown, to water.

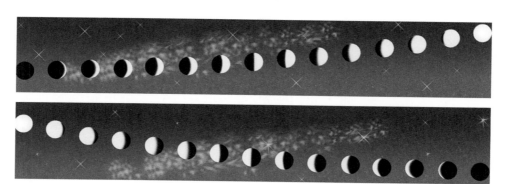

Top: The New Moon, invisible in the sky, waxes through crescent, First Quarter (half moon), gibbous to Full Moon, getting bigger every day, until it appears as a full circle.
Bottom: The round Full Moon wanes through gibbous, Last Quarter (half moon), crescent, and ends with the New Moon.

Tradition and the Moon

The Moon, being an ever-changing heavenly body, has always intrigued humans. We have long looked for connections between its phases and weather forecasts, health, births, animals and plants. For example, mushrooms can rarely be found at the time of the New Moon, even if the season and moisture are favourable, as this is their gestating period. They begin to appear on the fifth day of the lunar phase cycle and will be magnificently tender and succulent at the time of the Full Moon, or a little earlier. As the Moon wanes, their growth slows down and they gradually dry out.

Constellations of the Zodiac

Going back to prehistory, humans studied the stars. The first records come from the Chaldeans who could read the time of night in the sky, orient themselves and follow the seasons.

Lunar months or periods

There are four major lunar periods, each about a month in length.

Sidereal period

As we saw above, the sidereal period is the time it takes for the Moon to return to the same star in its revolution around the Earth. It is 27 days, 7 hours, 43 minutes and 12 seconds.

Synodic period

The synodic period refers to the phases of the Moon. As early as the third century BC, Babylonians had precisely calculated the average duration between two similar lunar phases (for example, two Full Moons) to an accuracy of 5 seconds. The average duration of the synodic period is 29 days, 12 hours, 44 minutes and 3 seconds.

Anomalistic (or apsidal) period

In its elliptical orbit the Moon is sometimes further from the Earth (apogee) and sometimes closer (perigee). The time from one perigee (or apogee) to the next is 27 days, 13 hours, 18 minutes and 33 seconds on average.

Draconitic (or nodal) revolution

The Moon's path through the stars does not exactly follow the Sun's path (the ecliptic). Its orbit is inclined by about 5 degrees to the ecliptic, crossing it twice at 'nodes'. The ascending node is where the Moon crosses from south of the ecliptic to north. The descending node is where it crosses from north of the ecliptic to south. The time between successive passages of the Moon through the same nodes is 27 days, 5 hours, 5 minutes and 36 seconds.

The twelve constellations

The 'fixed stars' have a constant relationship to each other even though they move across the sky, some rising and setting. Since ancient times these fixed stars have been seen in groups or constellations. The Sun, the Moon and the planets continually travel through a band of these fixed stars. This band consists of twelve constellations, which were seen as twelve animals or living beings in ancient Mesopotamia and Egypt. Hence the name *zodiac* (Greek *zoon*: animal, living being). You will always be able to pick out these constellations along the path followed by the Moon from the billions of stars surrounding us. The zodiac is a wide band of 18° around the line of the ecliptic, or ecliptic plane. Each star is a sun like ours. Some are much bigger than our Sun (Aldebaran, the most brilliant star in Taurus, has a diameter 36 times that of the Sun). Each of these stars, like our Sun, sends us its distant rays and we benefit from the influences of the constellation and its sky region. Let's take a look at these possible influences.

The precession of the equinoxes

Between March 20 and 22, depending on the year, the Sun crosses the celestial equator at the *vernal point*, marking the beginning of spring. This very specific point does not stay fixed in relation to the stars. It moves back every year by a 50 seconds of arc which comes to 1° over 72 years, or 30° over 2,160 years. This means that the vernal point which in Greek times was in the constellation of Aries, has now moved to the constellation of Pisces.

The Greeks divided the zodiac into twelve equal *signs* of 30° each. These *signs* are still used in astrology today. However for this calendar it is the visible *constellations* which are used. Because of the precession of the equinox the signs and constellations have shifted on average by one constellation.

The four elements

Just as a plant is composed of four parts – root, leaf, flower and fruit – the twelve zodiacal regions each have affinities with one of the main elements of the universe – earth, water, air and fire. These form four types of impulse regularly distributed around the Earth, and each impulse has a specific effect on particular parts of plants.

When it passes in front of a constellation, the Moon activates these different forces. It captures them, adds its own power then reflects them back to Earth just as it reflects the light of the Sun. Whenever gardeners work the soil, they make it more receptive to the influence of these elements.

The earth element

Attuned to the constellations of **Taurus, Virgo and Capricorn**, the earth element affects the buried part of the plant: the root. When the Moon passes in front of these earth constellations, it's the optimum time to enrich and prepare the soil, plant seeds, thin, weed, and transplant the seedlings of root vegetables. In particular, these constellations influence root and bulb crops such as garlic, onions, carrots, turnips, potatoes and radishes. When we respect this timing, these vegetables are more resistant to parasites

Constellations of the zodiac

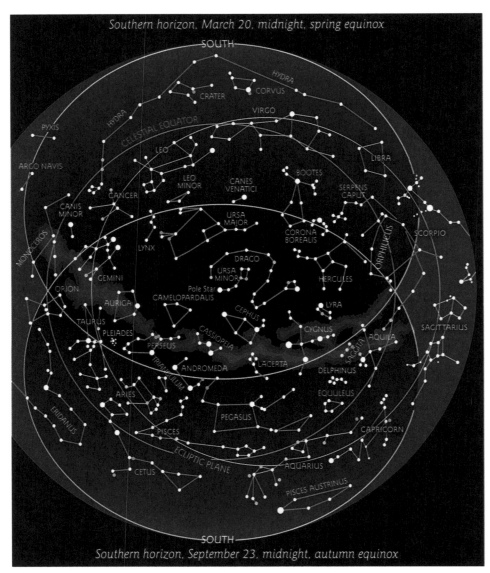

The top circular area of the illustration represents the sky at midnight on March 20, day of the spring equinox; the lower circular area, the sky at midnight on September 23, day of the autumn equinox. The constellations of the zodiac are along the ecliptic, the path followed every year by the Sun, and every month by the Moon.

when harvested, and their nutritional value, taste and productivity increase.

The water element

Active in **Cancer**, **Scorpio and Pisces**, the water element particularly influences moisture-loving parts of the plant: the stem and leaves.

Gardeners should use times when the Moon passes in front of water constellations to care for leaf and stem crops such as lettuce, spinach and asparagus. Doing so will yield beautiful, tender, crunchy leaves and delicate, tasty asparagus.

The air element

Due to its affinity with **Gemini**, **Libra** and **Aquarius**, the air element expresses itself in the fragrance of flowers, plants and vegetables. For optimum results, gardeners should use times when the Moon passes in front of air constellations to take care of flowers and flower crops such as artichokes, cauliflowers and broccoli.

The fire element

Related to **Aries**, **Leo** and **Sagittarius**, the fire element brings the warmth needed to ripen fruit and the seeds necessary for reproduction. Gardeners should use times when the Moon is in fire constellations to care for fruit and seed crops such as apricots, apples, peas, tomatoes and beans.

When gardening by element, be aware that some constellations are isolated, e.g. Gemini and Cancer, while others almost overlap, e.g. Taurus and Aries.

NOTE: The calendar gives very precise timings for the transition between ascending and descending moons (or vice versa), as well as for the passage between constellations. Gardeners should not rush to work as soon as it is 'the right time', for the effect is not instantaneous. Instead take time to think and plan the garden long-term. Also, remember that schedules are given for Greenwich Mean Time, so if you are not in Britain or Ireland you will need to make adjustments for local times (see p. 37).

Variable durations

The zodiac constellations are different lengths, which results in unequal time periods for gardening certain types of plant. In practice, this means that gardeners will always have more time for root vegetables than for flowers.
Earth constellations occupy:
Capricorn 28° + Taurus 36° + Virgo 46° = 110°
Water constellations: Pisces 38° + Cancer 21° + Scorpio 31° = 90°
Fire constellations: Sagittarius 30° + Aries 24° + Leo 35° = 89°
Air constellations: Aquarius 25° + Gemini 28° + Libra 18° = 71°

What if I can't always follow the Moon faithfully?

It's not always possible to strictly follow the Moon; it might be too cold, or just impossible to make time to garden. You can compensate by making sure you perform as many pre-harvest tasks at the most favourable time. If possible, prioritise the preparation and enrichment of soil, sowing and planting.

Current position of the zodiac constellations
and corresponding symbols in Western astrology

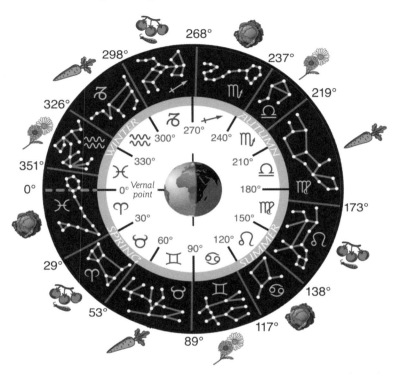

The inner circle shows the twelve signs of the zodiac as shown in horoscopes. In astrology, their size is a constant (30° each). The outer circle shows the constellations as they should be observed in gardening: for instance, the smallest constellation, Libra, covers 237°– 219° = 18°, not 30° as in astrology. **When you garden, make sure you follow the actual duration of each constellation as our calendar does.**

Zodiac constellations	♈ Aries	♌ Taurus	♐ Sagittarius
	♉ Taurus	♍ Virgo	♑ Capricorn
	♊ Gemini	♎ Libra	♒ Aquarius
	♋ Cancer	♏ Scorpio	♓ Pisces

Explanation of gardening symbols

LEAF	FLOWER	ROOT	SEED & FRUIT
Water constellations	Air constellations	Earth constellations	Fire constellations

Lunar Irregularities

There are times when the Moon does not provide the optimum conditions for gardening, specifically during periods of significant lunar change. Be sure to wait 5 hours either side of a moon node, apogee or perigee before gardening and, if possible, wait even longer if there is an eclipse.

Perigee and apogee

The Moon travels on an elliptical orbit, in which the centre of Earth is one of the foci. Every lunar month, the Moon passes through the **perigee**, the point where its distance from the Earth is smallest (356,500 km/221,500 miles) and its speed greatest (moving 15° per day). Conversely, at the **apogee**, the Moon is at its most distant point (406,700 km /252,700 miles) and its speed is at its slowest (moving 12° per day). Gardening during the Moon's perigee can result in weak and sickly plants, while vegetation can be shrunken, constricted and prone to sickness when planted during the apogee.

If the Full Moon or the New Moon coincide with the perigee, there is an even greater likelihood of irregularities, particularly if it coincides with an equinox or solstice. This was the case during Storm Martin, which violently swept across Europe in December 1999. Likewise, the devastating tsunami of December 2004 took place at the time of the winter solstice, on the eve of the Moon's apogee on December 27.

To avoid a weak harvest, watch out for these situations: Sun at the time of equinox or solstice + Full Moon, and New Moon at the perigee.

Moon nodes

The plane of the Moon's orbit is at an angle of 5.1° from the plane of the ecliptic, along which the Sun travels. The Moon crosses this plane twice every month, at two points called nodes. (The ascending node is when the Moon crosses from south of the ecliptic to north. The descending node is where it crosses from north of the ecliptic to south.) When the Full Moon or New Moon coincides with a node, there is an eclipse of the Moon or the Sun. Plants are particularly sensitive at these times, so keep in mind that sowing will produce sterile seeds. You may also often notice that the sky is white during a moon node. Again, it is best not to garden 5 hours before or after this point.

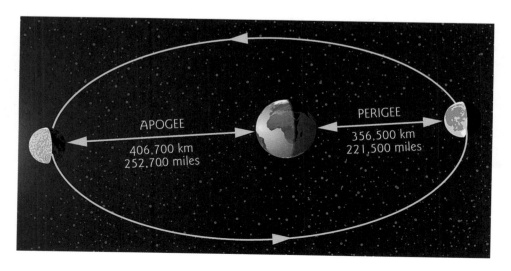

APOGEE
406,700 km
252,700 miles

PERIGEE
356,500 km
221,500 miles

The Moon after Easter

While the true power of the Moon is constantly being discussed and argued, in agriculture the influence of the Moon after Easter has always been unquestioned. The most ancient texts bear witness to it, and gardeners still watch out for its coming.

Easter always occurs after the Full Moon after the spring equinox. At this time of year, the Sun is already high and the days last longer. When the sky is clear, daytime temperatures begin to rise, allowing small seedlings and budding fruit to soak up the warmth. After sunset, the cold returns and the thermometer dips; gradually a cold dew covers the plants and it can sometimes still be frosty at dawn. Young plants can often suffer during these cold nights, so keep any weather protection in place during this time.

Eclipses

If the New Moon occurs near a node (see p. 19) there is a solar eclipse. If the Full Moon coincides with a node, there will be a lunar eclipse. Plants are extremely sensitive to these phenomena, so it is advisable to avoid gardening during these times.

Moon nodes

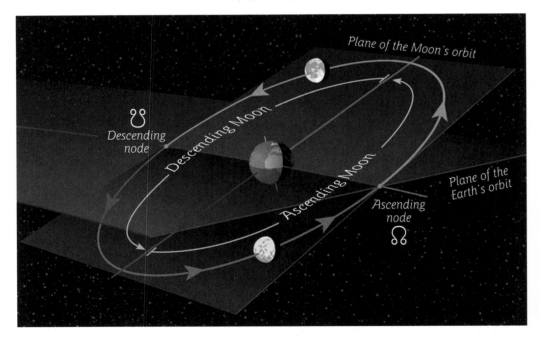

The Moon and Plants

Every type of plant is affected differently by the Moon's position in each constellation. Vegetables can be classified as root, leaf, flower or fruit depending on the plant part we consume. For example, beetroot, onion and potatoes are all roots; chard, cabbage and Brussels sprouts are leaves; artichokes and broccoli are flowers; and tomatoes, aubergine (or eggplant) and peas are fruit, as are grains and fruit trees.

Root, leaf, flower or fruit?

Below is a partial list of vegetables, ornamental plants and fruit trees.
Adapt the list to match what you plan to cultivate.

Root	Leaf	Flower	Seed and Fruit
Beet(root)	Asparagus	Broccoli	Aubergine (eggplant)
Carrot	Brussels sprout	Cauliflower	Berries
Celeriac	Cabbage	Globe artichoke	Broad bean (fava)
Chervil (root)	Cardoon		Chilli pepper
Chicory*	Celery	Flowering bushes	Courgette (zucchini)
Chinese artichoke	Chicory*	– Forsythia	Cucumber
Garlic	Cress	– Lilac	Fruit trees
Horseradish	Dandelion	– Magnolia	Green bean
Jerusalem artichoke	Endive*	– Rose	Lentils
Leek	Fennel	– Wisteria	Melon
Onion	Grass		Peas
Parsnip	Herbs	Flowers	Pepper
Potato	Lettuce	– Annuals	Strawberry
Radish	Lamb's lettuce	– Biennials	Squash
Salsify	(mâche)	– Bulbs	Tomato
Shallot	Ornamental bushes	– Perennials	Watermelon
Swede (rutabaga)	Purslane		
Turnip	Rhubarb		Grains
	Rocket (arugula)		– Barley
	Romaine lettuce		– Corn
	Sorrel		– Oats
	Spinach		– Rye
	Swiss chard		– Wheat

NOTE: *The cultivation of endive and chicory has two stages. The aim with the original seeding is to produce strong roots, so sow the seed in an ascending moon, on a root day. Pull them up, again on a root day, and let them dry a few days on the ground. The second stage – forcing – aims to produce beautiful leaves, ideal for cooking or salads. This is achieved by replanting the roots and harvesting the leaves on leaf days.*

Gardening According to the Moon's Position

In order to benefit from the influence of the Moon, particular types of plants should be sown according to whether the Moon is ascending or descending, and which constellation it is passing through. For example, by looking at the grid below we can see that lettuce (a leaf crop) is best sown in an ascending moon when the Moon is in Pisces, and that forsythia (a flower) should be planted in a descending moon when the Moon passes in front of Gemini or Libra.

Movement of the Moon	Constellation/ element	Type of plant	Task
Ascending	Sagittarius ♐ Fire 30°	Seed and fruit	In the ascending Moon:
Ascending	Capricorn ♑ Earth 28°	Root	• Sow • Harvest leaves (spinach, lettuce)
Ascending	Aquarius ♒ Air 25°	Flower	• Harvest flowers (artichokes)
Ascending	Pisces ♓ Water 38°	Leaf	• Harvest fruit (tomatoes, peas, apples)
Ascending	Aries ♈ Fire 24°	Seed and fruit	• Cut transplants and graft
Ascending	Taurus ♉ Earth 36°	Root	
Ascending	Gemini ♊ Air 28°	Flower	

Movement of the Moon	Constellation/ element	Type of plant	Task
Descending	Gemini ♊ Air 28°	Flower	In the descending Moon:
Descending	Cancer ♋ Water 21°	Leaf	• Propagate from cuttings
Descending	Leo ♌ Fire 35°	Seed and fruit	• Enrich the soil • Thin seedlings • Transplant seedlings
Descending	Virgo ♍ Earth 46°	Root	• Harvest roots (carrots, turnips)
Descending	Libra ♎ Air 18°	Flower	• Prune and pinch back
Descending	Scorpio ♏ Water 31°	Leaf	• Divide plants • Layer
Descending	Sagittarius ♐ Fire 30°	Seed and fruit	

The descending Moon ends in Gemini and the ascending Moon starts in Sagittarius. Following our calendar allows you to match your garden activities with the movement of the Moon in the sky.

Plants in their Environment

As a living being fixed in the soil, a plant is entirely dependent on its environment. On one hand, it raises its stem towards the sky to catch the light and warmth of the Sun, while on the other, it plunges its roots into the Earth looking for everything it needs to grow and reproduce. Food, water, minerals and cosmic life forces are all essential to a plant's survival, and the condition of the soil is vitally important in ensuring these resources are successfully delivered.

Cosmic forces

We can aid plants' sensitivity to cosmic influences by doing all we can to increase their receptiveness. Suppressing artificial obstacles to cosmic forces, making the atmosphere permeable, and introducing easily assimilated food into the soil all help to optimise plants' sensitivity. By making the helpful cosmic forces as accessible as possible, we will see the benefit in the roots, leaves, flowers and fragrances of our gardens.

Most cosmic forces, in particular those of the Moon, act only indirectly on plants; before roots can take them in, they are absorbed by the soil – depending on its receptivity and the current position in the lunar cycle. The health and vigour of our vegetables call for well-balanced, aerated and receptive soil.

Soil

In order to develop properly, plants need air, light and soil in which to take root and absorb water and nutrients. These elements are more easily available to plants when the soil's fertility has been restored with beneficial manures and enrichments, which are active during the most favourable lunar dates.

Every soil is different; whether sandy, clay or lime, it will need to be loosened regularly and be fertilised with appropriate growth aids and enlivening manures. **Ensure chemical fertilisers are not used:** besides their harmful effect on crops, they make the soil impervious to the influence of cosmic forces. When gardening with the Moon, feed soil exclusively with well-ripened compost, animal manure, green manures and liquid slurries of vitalising plants, for example nettles and comfrey. Soil should not remain bare between two crops: depending on the season, sow clover, rye, vetch or mustard to contribute helpful organic matter and protect the soil from weathering (see 'Growing green manures' and 'Mulching' p. 26–27).

Air and light

Sunlight is integral to a plant's development. Gardeners should make sure that their growing space has the maximum amount of light, but shouldn't hesitate to plant a hedge of mixed bushes on the side of the prevailing wind for protection. The hedge will filter the air, protecting plants from chemical treatments which might have been applied in neighbouring properties, and will also shelter birds that feed on aphids, caterpillars and unwanted insects.

Improving and feeding the soil

Gardeners who use the Moon can also make the most of their soil by following the general principles of biodynamic gardening (see Further Reading, p. 119). Work the soil without disrupting the direction of the top layer, and improve it with natural matter that will be organically assimilated by the plants on decomposing. Year on year, this will gradually improve the fertility of the soil, enabling the successful growth of healthy vegetables, flowers and fruit.

Working the soil

Soil is alive. It contains millions of micro-organisms invisible to the eye, as well as being home to bigger inhabitants such as earthworms and beetles. On the soil's surface, we find aerobic micro-organisms that need oxygen to survive, while anaerobic organisms live deeper down. Whenever the soil is ploughed, by hand or machine, the top layers are inverted, together with the micro-organisms they contain, which subsequently often die. Yet these minuscule creatures and bacteria are a gardener's allies. They break down organic matter, transforming it into humus, which plants can then use for food and growth.

With this in mind, it is vital that we adopt 'soft' practices for aerating the soil, without disturbing it. Adapted hand cultivators should be used where possible (consisting of two handles connected by a bar at the bottom, in which three to five vertical tines are inserted) and soil should be worked while walking backwards. Plunging the tines into the soil and lowering the handles produces a crumbly, aerated soil, which will in turn create a loose, aerated growing surface.

Making compost

Waste from the garden and kitchen can be turned into excellent compost. Dry or brown garden waste, including bush cuttings (crushed first, if possible) and dead leaves, and green and wet waste from lawn mowing, weeds and vegetable peelings can all be used to create homemade compost. Plants that have gone to seed, sick plants or vegetation affected by parasites (whether eggs, larvae or fully formed) should be avoided, in addition to rose cuttings, fruit-tree leaves and wormy fruit. Waste should be piled up in a corner of the garden or in a composter, alternating dry and wet matter in layers approximately 25 cm (10 in) thick. Ideally, the waste should touch the ground to allow earthworms to rise into the pile and break everything down. You can speed up the process by adding earth worms, which will digest your waste. If necessary, water the pile once a month to hasten the process further, and make sure you cover the pile to keep it warm, which will speed up fermentation. Your compost will be ripe in approximately 10 months. Use it at the end of winter, incorporating it superficially into the soil, spreading it between flowers, in the planting holes of 'greedy' vegetables, fruit trees or berry bushes, and in the mixture you use to repot any potted plants.

Introducing natural fertilisers

More and more garden centres sell 'natural fertilisers' containing the same elements as chemical fertilisers: nitrogen (N), phosphorus (P) and potassium (K). The nitrogen often comes from feather meal, horns and castor-oil cake, while phosphorus is provided by fish bones, natural phosphate and beet stillage. They decompose slowly and are absorbed gradually, feeding the soil, renewing its fertility and gently nourishing the plants without harming them. However, natural fertilisers must be introduced ahead of growing time, either in autumn or late winter when the soil is being prepared. Recommended dosages will be indicated on the product package and should be adhered to. More specific fertilisers can be added later in the growing cycle for demanding crops, but dried blood and guano should be avoided: their rapid action is similar to that of chemical fertilisers and they have a tendency to leach out when it rains.

Growing green manures

Green manures are sown specifically to improve the structure of the soil; to enrich and cover it so that it won't get packed when it rains, in addition to fighting some parasites and weeds. When choosing green manure crops, consider the duration of their growth cycle, their uses and the nature of your soil. Green manures find their place between the harvest of one crop and the seeding or planting of another in the same patch, if there is a long gap, for instance between spring spinach and autumn turnips. You can also use them in late summer and autumn in a bed you plan to keep fallow until next spring. In the latter case, the crop will have to be frost hardy. Green manures not killed by frost should be cut back after they bloom to make sure they don't reseed themselves, then crushed and buried. Do not plant a green manure crop of the same family as the vegetable that precedes or follows it (see table and 'Crop Rotation' p. 28).

Sweet lupins are sown from March to July (1–2 kg/100 m^2, 2–4 lb/100 sq yd). The white lupin prefers heavy soils, while the yellow lupin likes poor, sandy soil.

White mustard is sown from March to August (150–200 g/100 m^2, 4–6 oz/100 sq yd) but should not be grown immediately before or after cabbages, turnips or radishes. It is good for heavy, even limey soil and grows quickly, fighting nematodes and weeds.

Phacelia can be sown from March to August (150–200 g/100 m^2, 4–6 oz/100 sq yd) and should be buried two months later. Phacelia grows very quickly, fights nematodes and its flowers attract numerous pollinators. There are no vegetables in this plant family so it can be grown between any variety.

Buckwheat should be sown from May to August (500–600 g/100 m^2, 14–18 oz/100 sq yd) as this crop is not frost hardy. It is especially useful when used in poor acid soils to loosen soil and choke weeds.

Rye can be sown in September or October (2 kg/100 m^2, 4 lb/100 sq. yards). Completely hardy, it should be buried in spring. Suited to poor soils on the acidic side and for fighting weeds, rye can also be grown together with vetch (500 g/1lb rye and 700 g/1.5 lb vetch per 100 m² /100 sq yd. The latter's tendrils hang on to its stems, and this combination has been found to improve nitrogen content in the soil.

White clover is sown from April to September (50–100 g/100 m², 1.5–3 oz/ 100 sq. yards) in cold heavy soils. Dig it under in autumn and spring, and remember that this perennial can also be grown in paths.

Mulching
Another way to keep soil covered between crops is to spread mulch over empty beds. This keeps the soil cool between rainfall or watering, and slows the growth of weeds, making them easier to pull. Some mulches can also enrich or lighten soil, but **wait until the earth warms up in spring before adding them, preferably in May.**
   Prepare the soil by weeding carefully and watering, before spreading a 5 cm (2 in) layer of mulch on top, which can include grass mowings, hemp or linen chaff, cocoa shells or crushed straw. The layer should be renewed regularly, as grass mowings break down particularly fast. Spread the mulch at the end of spring, and turn it in autumn.

Choosing plants and their location

Over the years, gardeners have come to notice that some plants help each other out – they are 'companions'– whereas others seem to 'dislike' each other. These affinities can be used when planning your garden, and if successfully paired, your vegetables and other plants will be stronger as a result and more resistant to parasites and disease. Taking the time to establish yearly rotations and companion plants can also help avoid the need for chemical treatments. This process becomes easier as time passes, and you will be well rewarded. Remember that some vegetables need to be pollinated, so sow them next to plants that attract honeybees.

Attracting pollinators
Bees and other pollinating insects are becoming rarer, despite their usefulness. To encourage their presence in your garden, sow or plant borage, cosmos flowers, marigolds, phacelia or calendula along garden paths and between vegetable rows. Choose simple flowers, which make foraging easier, and when planting herbs, plant more of them than you need so you can allow some to bloom. Pollinators love chives, rosemary, savoury and thyme, and as they visit them, they will also visit vegetable flowers nearby – aubergine (eggplant), cucumber, squash, strawberries, beans, peas and tomatoes – making for a more abundant harvest.

Choosing companion plants
Although it is not entirely clear how, some plants seem to encourage their neighbours' growth. This is certainly the case with borage, nasturtium, marigold, sage and sunflowers. These plants also attract pollinating insects and repel parasites, so plant them throughout your garden (see table on p. 29).

Crop rotation

The term 'crop rotation' refers to the succession of crops on the same plot of garden. It is determined by plants' own cycles, rather than by the calendar year. Here's an example of how to implement crop rotation in a vegetable garden:

Year 1: divide your vegetable garden into four squares of the same surface area. **In square 1**, sow legumes such as peas and beans that contribute nitrogen to the soil. After the harvest, cut the stems so that they decompose in the ground. **In square 2**, plant leaf vegetables such as cabbage, lettuce and spinach. In **square 3** plant roots: potatoes, beets, turnips and so on. **Divide square 4 in two:** keep one half fertiliser-free for undemanding plants such as bulbs (garlic, shallot, onion); in the other half, incorporate compost and plant or sow vegetables that need a rich soil, for example aubergine (eggplant), cucumber, squash, melons, tomatoes and flower crop (broccoli, cauliflower etc.).

In the following years, rotate the vegetables in the squares:
Year 2: In square 1, leaf vegetables replace legumes, benefiting from the nitrogen left behind. **In square 2**, root vegetables follow leaves, looking for food deeper in the soil. **Square 3** will be divided: one half for demanding, the other half for undemanding vegetables. Cultivate legumes in **square 4**.
In years 3 and 4, keep shifting crops around the squares, always in the same order. **In year 5** cultivate the same vegetables in the same squares as in year 1.

Some plants remain in place for several seasons (perennial herbs, artichokes, asparagus, strawberries, small fruit, rhubarb etc.) on the edges of the garden and along paths. Place them a little to the north and west depending on their sun requirements, so that they won't overshadow the crops.

A few location rules

In summary, following these simple rules will help prevent deficiencies and disease:

- **Respect individual plants' preferences** regarding soil fertility (some plants are greedy, others less demanding or downright abstemious) and the acid or alkaline nature of the soil.
- **Consider 'companion planting'**– favourable or unfavourable proximities (see table on p. 29)
- **Practise crop rotation** – avoid cultivating plants of the same family in the same location two years in a row (see table below).

Green manure plants

Plant family	Herbs, grains, vegetables	Green manures
Apiaceae	carrot, celery, chervil, fennel, parsnip, parsley	
Asteraceae	artichoke, cardoon, chicory, tarragon, lettuce, salsify	
Brassica	cabbage, cress, white turnip, radish, horseradish, rocket	rape, white mustard, brassica
Chenopodiaceae	beets, spinach, Swiss chard	
Cucurbitaceae	cucumber, squash, melon, watermelon, pumpkin	
Fabaceae	beans, lentils, peas	lupin, alfalfa, sainfoin, clover, vetch

Plant family	Herbs, grains, vegetables	Green manures
Hydrophyllaceae		phacelia
Lamiaceae	basil, Chinese artichoke, mint, oregano, rosemary, sage, thyme	
Liliaceae	garlic, asparagus, chive, shallot, onion, leek	
Poaceae	oats, wheat, corn, barley, rye	oat, rye
Polygonaceae	sorrel, rhubarb	buckwheat
Solanaceae	aubergine (eggplant), pepper, potato, tomato	

Companion planting

As discussed, plants influence each other when grown together; some encourage growth, while others dislike being in close proximity. It is well known that leeks keep away the carrot fly, the proximity of carrots discourages leek moths, and radishes are sweeter when grown near lettuce. The table below will help you to discover other associations and which crops to separate.

✓: friends
✗: enemies

	asparagus	aubergine (eggplant)	beet(root)	broad bean (fava)	cabbage	carrot	celery	cucumber	garlic	green bean	leek	lettuce	melon	onion	pea	potato	pumpkin	radish	shallot	spinach	squash/courgette	strawberry	tomato	turnip
asparagus							✓	✓		✓	✓	✓			✓									
aubergine (eggplant)								✓									✓	✓					✓	
beet(root)				✓	✗	✓				✓	✓	✗		✓	✗			✓	✓	✓			✗	
broad bean (fava)					✓	✓	✓	✓	✗	✓	✗	✓		✗	✗	✓		✓	✗	✓		✓		
cabbage			✓	✓		✓	✓	✓		✓		✓		✗	✓	✓		✗	✗	✓		✗		
carrot			✗	✓	✓		✓			✓	✓	✓		✓	✓	✗		✓	✓	✓			✓	
celery			✓	✓	✓	✓		✓		✓	✓	✗		✓	✗								✓	
cucumber	✓			✓	✓	✓				✓		✓	✗	✓	✗								✗	
garlic	✓		✓	✗	✓					✗	✗				✗			✓					✗	
green bean	✓	✓	✓	✓	✓	✓	✓	✓	✗		✓	✓		✗	✗			✓	✓	✓		✓		✓
leek	✓	✓	✗	✗	✓	✓		✗				✓		✓	✗	✗		✓		✓		✓	✓	✓
lettuce	✓		✓	✓	✓	✗	✓	✓		✓	✓			✓	✓	✓		✓	✓	✓	✓	✓		✓
melon						✗				✓					✓			✓	✗					
onion			✓	✗	✗	✓		✓		✗	✓	✓			✗	✗		✓				✓	✓	✗
pea	✓		✗	✓	✓	✓			✗	✗	✗	✓	✓	✗		✓		✓	✗	✓			✗	✓
potato			✗	✓	✓	✗	✗	✗	✓	✓				✗	✗		✗	✓			✗		✗	
pumpkin		✓														✗		✓						
radish		✓	✓	✓	✗	✓	✓			✓		✓			✓						✓	✗		
shallot			✓	✗	✗	✓				✗		✓									✗	✗	✓	
spinach			✓	✓	✓	✓				✓	✓	✓		✓				✓				✓	✓	✓
squash/courgette				✓						✓		✓	✗	✓		✗							✗	
strawberry				✗						✓	✓	✓		✓				✓	✓				✓	
tomato	✓		✗		✓	✓	✗	✓		✓				✓	✗	✗		✓	✓	✓	✓	✗		✓
turnip										✓		✓		✗	✓					✓			✓	

Fighting disease and parasites

Don't reach for the spray pump the minute you spot aphids or powdery mildew. Take preventive action by encouraging the development of helpful insects, introducing companion plants whose fragrance repels parasites, or using plant-based preparations. Pesticides should only be used as a last resort.

Encouraging helpful insects

Learn to recognise not only adult insects but also their eggs and larvae, so as not to destroy them mistakenly. Ladybirds, hoverflies and lacewings are your allies and will devour aphids. If you plant nectar-rich flowers and provide natural or manmade shelters where they can spend the winter, these helpful creatures will be ready for action as soon as the first pests appear in spring. Most importantly, use chemical treatments as little as possible. If aphids appear before their predators, cut back the affected parts of the plant, giving the helpful insects time to develop ahead of the next generation of pests.

Making plant preparations

Herbal preparations are made by macerating certain plants before they go to seed and spraying the resulting 'tea' to fight disease or parasites. Always use rainwater and wooden containers (never metal), preferably closed, to mix preparations. Since these liquids do not keep very long, be ready to prepare several batches in the course of a growing season.

Two techniques are used: manures (or macerations) and teas (or decoctions). **For manures**, soak the plants in cold water until all soluble substances are dissolved, then filter and dilute the manure before use. You can use ferns to fight aphids and slugs; nettles against aphids and various diseases; and elder to fight flea beetles, aphids and thrips, and to prevent as well as fight cabbage white butterflies and leek moths. **For teas**, soak plants for an entire day, then boil over a low heat for 20 minutes, allow to cool, then filter for use. Horsetail is good for all diseases, while tansy is effective for aphids, cutworms and cabbage white butterflies.

Recipes

Nettle manure

Macerate 1 kg (2 lb) fresh, chopped nettles in 10 l (qt) rain water for 4–5 days. Filter and dilute to 20% (2 parts) manure to 10 parts water) before spraying.

Elder manure

Chop 1 kg (2 lb) elder leaves, flowers, fruit and young stems. Soak in 10 l (qt) water for 3 days. Filter but don't dilute.

Horsetail tea

Cut 200 g (8 oz) fresh horsetail leaves and mix with 10 l (qt) water. Soak for 1 day before boiling for 20 minutes. Let it rest for 24 hours, then filter before spraying.

Establishing insect-repellent plants

The smell of many plants' leaves repels parasites and some diseases. Other plants attract them, pulling them away from neighbouring vegetables or ornamental plants. Below is a table of approximately 20 plant-allies and the parasites and diseases they fight.

Helpful plants	Use for	Plant near
Garlic, chives, shallots, onion	blister beetle flies	peach tree carrot
Lovage	flea beetle aphids	cabbage, turnip, radish beans, lettuce, tomato
Basil	mildew	cucumber, squash
Borage	cabbage white butterfly	cabbage
Nasturtium	whitefly mildew aphids	aubergine (eggplant), cabbage, cucumber, tomato tomato cabbage, cucumber, squash, beans, lettuce, pepper, roses, tomato
Chives	Japanese beetle flies	potato carrot
Coriander (cilantro)	flea beetle Japanese beetle flies	beets, cabbage, turnip, radish potato carrot
Cosmos	cabbage white butterfly	cabbage
Lettuce	flea beetle	cabbage, turnip, radish
Lavender	aphids	roses
Mint	flea beetle cabbage white butterfly	cabbage, turnip radish cabbage
French marigold	whitefly flea beetle nematodes cabbage white butterfly aphids	aubergine (eggplant), cabbage, cucumber, tomato cabbage, turnip, radish tomato cabbage cucumber, squash, spinach, beans, pepper
Parsley	flies aphids	carrot, onion melon, tomato
Horseradish	Japanese beetle rust	potato celery
Rosemary	flea beetle flies cabbage white butterfly aphids	cabbage, turnip, radish carrot, bean cabbage beans, lettuce
Savory	flea beetle flies cabbage white butterfly aphids	cabbage, turnip, radish beans cabbage beans, lettuce
Sage	flea beetle flies cabbage white butterfly aphids	cabbage, turnip, radish carrot cabbage cucumber, squash, lettuce
Common marigold	whitefly nematodes aphids	aubergine (eggplant), cabbage, cucumber, tomato tomato squash, spinach, lettuce, beans, peppers
Tobacco	whitefly thrips	aubergine (eggplant), cabbage, cucumber, tomato gladiolus, pea
Thyme	flea beetle slugs cabbage white butterfly	cabbage, turnip, radish squash, spinach, lettuce, melon cabbage
Tomato	flea beetle	cabbage, turnip, radish

Designing your Garden

You can use the space below to design your garden. If your growing space is small, draw the layout of your March–April crops on the left and your June–July crops on the right, after you have harvested the spring yield.

Indicate where the north lies in relation to your garden. Include unchanging elements such as walls, hedges, paths, cold frames, perennials, fruit trees, herbs, asparagus and artichokes. If these aren't in place yet, indicate where they will be, and pay attention to any tall, overshadowing plants.

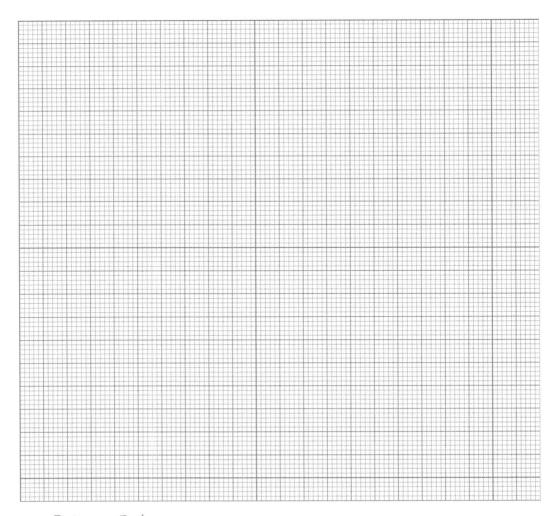

Divide the remaining surface into four equally-sized sections, which will each be occupied by one of the four main categories of vegetable: root, leaf, flower, seed and fruit (see p. 21). Plan the location of your winter crops according to the rules of crop rotation, companion planting and integrating flowers, indicating where the beds will be. When the time is right, just follow your plans and sow or plant your seedlings.

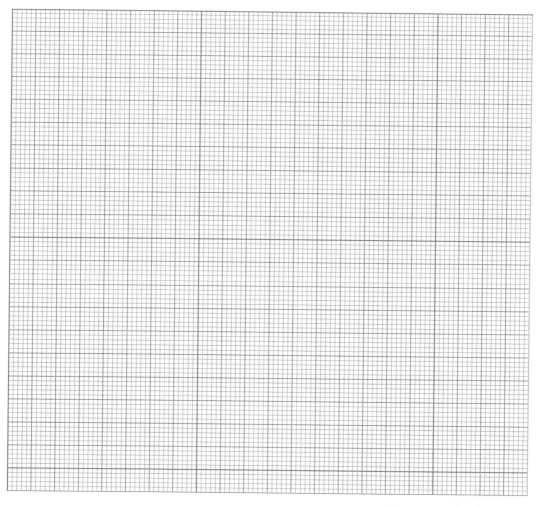

2018
Calendar

How to Use the Calendar

On the following pages, you will find a calendar for the Northern hemisphere and Greenwich Mean Time. It takes into account the main influences from the cosmos, as described in the chapter 'The Moon and the Garden' (pp. 8–33). The vegetables and plants listed are chosen as examples that suit the average growing conditions in France, and can be varied according to your taste, the climate of your garden and its latitude and altitude. Each day we suggest example tasks for tending to leaves, roots, flowers or fruit, according to season, the position of the Sun, and the position of the Moon (ascending or descending in front of particular constellations). You will have to protect your crops from the cold or the heat depending on the climate of your garden and the time of year. The examples given match an *average* climate in France. Take into account your own climate, jumping ahead or postponing tasks as compared to the calendar. If you have frost, delay all planting, pruning and treatments.

Note

It is not always possible – for personal or climatic reasons – to choose the best moment to perform particular gardening tasks. The main consideration should be the motion of the Moon – **always sow when the moon is ascending, plant and prune when the Moon is descending.**

We have included a blank page every two weeks for you to keep a daily journal. Note everything you do in the garden: which variety of carrots or beans you sow, which day the lettuce came up, when you picked the first tomatoes or beans, when the almond tree blossomed, and when the first cuckoo sang. Don't hesitate to include birthdays. Does someone like a particular plant? Make a note in your calendar to sow or plant this flower at the right time so you can give them a cutting. Your notes will help you to progress your gardening skills and knowledge, and the more notes you take, the more pleasure you will have consulting them.

Remember, all times are given in GMT. If you are not in Britain or Ireland, you need to adjust for your time zone (see p. 37).

Crop tables

You may prefer to plan your tasks differently. Make a list of the plants you want to cultivate and then create a personal calendar of your gardening with the Moon. The crop table on pp. 106–15 offers a range of possibilities.

Calendar key

⊙   the Sun
⊙ ♐   e.g. the Sun is in Sagittarius
      (see p. 18 for constellation symbols)
○   full Moon
◑   first quarter Moon
●   new Moon
◐   last quarter Moon
☊   ascending Moon node
☋   descending Moon node

Note: Do not confuse ascending or descending Moon nodes with the ascending or descending Moon.

Local Times

Times given are *Greenwich Mean Time* (GMT), using 24-hour clock, e.g. 3pm is written 15:00. **No account is taken of daylight saving (summer) time (DST).** Note 00:00 is midnight at the beginning of a date, and 24:00 is midnight at the end of the date. Add (+) or subtract (−) times as below. For countries not listed check local time against GMT.

Europe

Britain, Ireland, Portugal: GMT
    (March 25 to Oct 27, $+1^h$ for DST)
Iceland: GMT (no DST)
Central Europe: $+1^h$
    (March 25 to Oct 27, $+2^h$ for DST)
Eastern Europe (Finland, etc.): $+2^h$
    (March 25 to Oct 27, $+3^h$ for DST)
Russia (Moscow), Georgia: $+4^h$ (no DST)

Africa/Asia

Egypt: add 2^h (no DST)
Israel: add 2^h (March 23 to Oct 27,
    $+3^h$ for DST)
India: add $5\frac{1}{2}^h$ (no DST)
Philippines, China: add 8^h (no DST)
Japan, Korea: add 9^h (no DST)

North America

Newfoundland Standard Time: $-3\frac{1}{2}^h$
    (March 11 to Nov 3, $-2\frac{1}{2}^h$ for DST)
Atlantic Standard Time: -4^h
    (March 11 to Nov 3, -3^h for DST)
Eastern Standard Time: -5^h
    (March 11 to Nov 3, -4^h for DST)
Central Standard Time: -6^h
    (except Saskatchewan March 11 to Nov 3,
    -5^h for DST)
Mountain Standard Time: -7^h (except AZ,
    March 11 to Nov 3, -6^h for DST)
Pacific Standard Time: -8^h
    (March 11 to Nov 3, -7^h for DST)
Alaska Standard Time: -9^h
    (March 11 to Nov 3, -8^h for DST)
Hawaii Standard Time: -10^h
    (no DST)
Mexico (CST): -6^h
    (April 1 to Oct 27, -5^h for DST)

January 2018

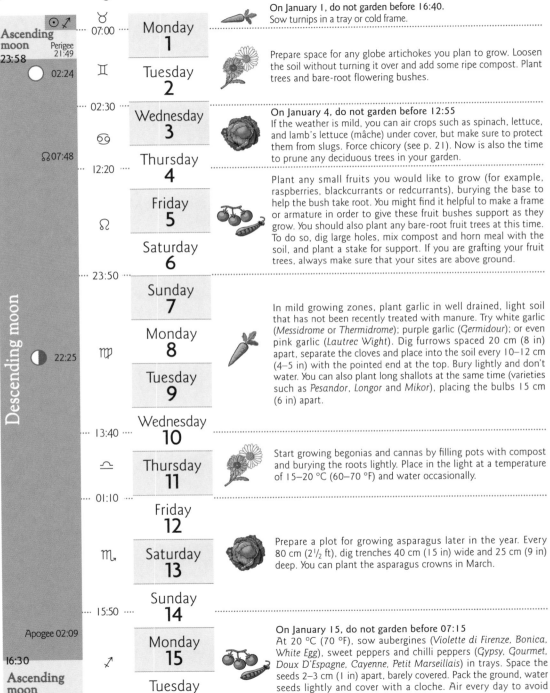

Ascending moon

23:58

Descending moon

Ascending moon

☉ ♐

Perigee
21:49

02:24

☊07:48

22:25

Apogee 02:09

16:30

07:00

02:30

12:20

23:50

13:40

01:10

15:50

♉

Ⅱ

♋

♌

♍

♎

♏

♐

Monday
1

Tuesday
2

Wednesday
3

Thursday
4

Friday
5

Saturday
6

Sunday
7

Monday
8

Tuesday
9

Wednesday
10

Thursday
11

Friday
12

Saturday
13

Sunday
14

Monday
15

Tuesday
16

On January 1, do not garden before 16:40.
Sow turnips in a tray or cold frame.

Prepare space for any globe artichokes you plan to grow. Loosen the soil without turning it over and add some ripe compost. Plant trees and bare-root flowering bushes.

On January 4, do not garden before 12:55
If the weather is mild, you can air crops such as spinach, lettuce, and lamb's lettuce (mâche) under cover, but make sure to protect them from slugs. Force chicory (see p. 21). Now is also the time to prune any deciduous trees in your garden.

Plant any small fruits you would like to grow (for example, raspberries, blackcurrants or redcurrants), burying the base to help the bush take root. You might find it helpful to make a frame or armature in order to give these fruit bushes support as they grow. You should also plant any bare-root fruit trees at this time. To do so, dig large holes, mix compost and horn meal with the soil, and plant a stake for support. If you are grafting your fruit trees, always make sure that your sites are above ground.

In mild growing zones, plant garlic in well drained, light soil that has not been recently treated with manure. Try white garlic (*Messidrome* or *Thermidrome*); purple garlic (*Germidour*); or even pink garlic (*Lautrec Wight*). Dig furrows spaced 20 cm (8 in) apart, separate the cloves and place into the soil every 10–12 cm (4–5 in) with the pointed end at the top. Bury lightly and don't water. You can also plant long shallots at the same time (varieties such as *Pesandor*, *Longor* and *Mikor*), placing the bulbs 15 cm (6 in) apart.

Start growing begonias and cannas by filling pots with compost and burying the roots lightly. Place in the light at a temperature of 15–20 °C (60–70 °F) and water occasionally.

Prepare a plot for growing asparagus later in the year. Every 80 cm (2½ ft), dig trenches 40 cm (15 in) wide and 25 cm (9 in) deep. You can plant the asparagus crowns in March.

On January 15, do not garden before 07:15
At 20 °C (70 °F), sow aubergines (*Violette di Firenze, Bonica, White Egg*), sweet peppers and chilli peppers (*Gypsy, Gourmet, Doux D'Espagne, Cayenne, Petit Marseillais*) in trays. Space the seeds 2–3 cm (1 in) apart, barely covered. Pack the ground, water seeds lightly and cover with a cloche. Air every day to avoid condensation.

Your notes and observations

January 2018

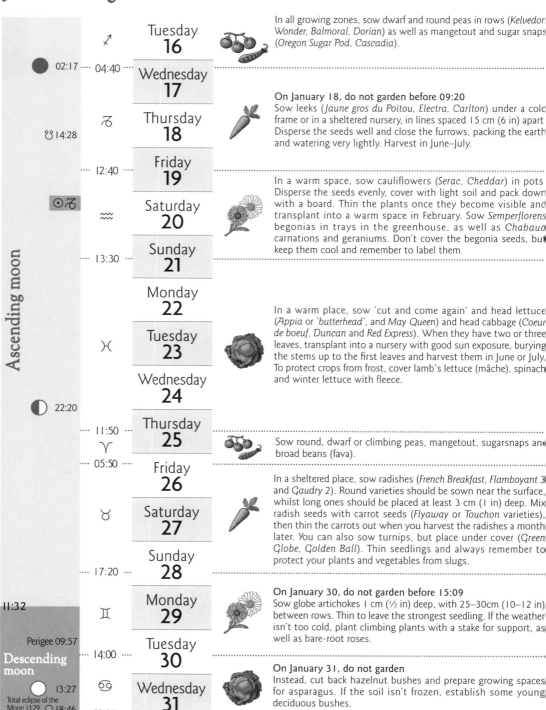

♐	Tuesday **16**	In all growing zones, sow dwarf and round peas in rows (*Kelvedon Wonder, Balmoral, Dorian*) as well as mangetout and sugar snaps (*Oregon Sugar Pod, Cascadia*).
● 02:17 ···· 04:40	Wednesday **17**	
♑ ℰ 14:28	Thursday **18**	**On January 18, do not garden before 09:20** Sow leeks (*Jaune gros du Poitou, Electra, Carlton*) under a cold frame or in a sheltered nursery, in lines spaced 15 cm (6 in) apart. Disperse the seeds well and close the furrows, packing the earth and watering very lightly. Harvest in June–July.
···· 12:40 ····	Friday **19**	
☉♑ ♒	Saturday **20**	In a warm space, sow cauliflowers (*Serac, Cheddar*) in pots. Disperse the seeds evenly, cover with light soil and pack down with a board. Thin the plants once they become visible and transplant into a warm space in February. Sow *Semperflorens* begonias in trays in the greenhouse, as well as *Chabaud* carnations and geraniums. Don't cover the begonia seeds, but keep them cool and remember to label them.
···· 13:30 ····	Sunday **21**	
	Monday **22**	In a warm place, sow 'cut and come again' and head lettuce (*Appia* or 'butterhead', and *May Queen*) and head cabbage (*Coeur de boeuf, Duncan* and *Red Express*). When they have two or three leaves, transplant into a nursery with good sun exposure, burying the stems up to the first leaves and harvest them in June or July. To protect crops from frost, cover lamb's lettuce (mâche), spinach and winter lettuce with fleece.
♓	Tuesday **23**	
	Wednesday **24**	
◐ 22:20	Thursday **25**	Sow round, dwarf or climbing peas, mangetout, sugarsnaps and broad beans (fava).
···· 11:50 ···· ♈ ···· 05:50 ····	Friday **26**	In a sheltered place, sow radishes (*French Breakfast, Flamboyant 3* and *Gaudry 2*). Round varieties should be sown near the surface, whilst long ones should be placed at least 3 cm (1 in) deep. Mix radish seeds with carrot seeds (*Flyaway* or *Touchon* varieties), then thin the carrots out when you harvest the radishes a month later. You can also sow turnips, but place under cover (*Green Globe, Golden Ball*). Thin seedlings and always remember to protect your plants and vegetables from slugs.
♉	Saturday **27**	
···· 17:20 ····	Sunday **28**	
11:32 Perigee 09:57	Monday **29**	**On January 30, do not garden before 15:09** Sow globe artichokes 1 cm (½ in) deep, with 25–30cm (10–12 in) between rows. Thin to leave the strongest seedling. If the weather isn't too cold, plant climbing plants with a stake for support, as well as bare-root roses.
Descending moon ♊ ···· 14:00 ····	Tuesday **30**	
○ 13:27 Total eclipse of the Moon 13:29 ♋ 18:46 ···· 23:30 ····	Wednesday **31** ♋	**On January 31, do not garden** Instead, cut back hazelnut bushes and prepare growing spaces for asparagus. If the soil isn't frozen, establish some young deciduous bushes.

Ascending moon

Your notes and observations

February 2018

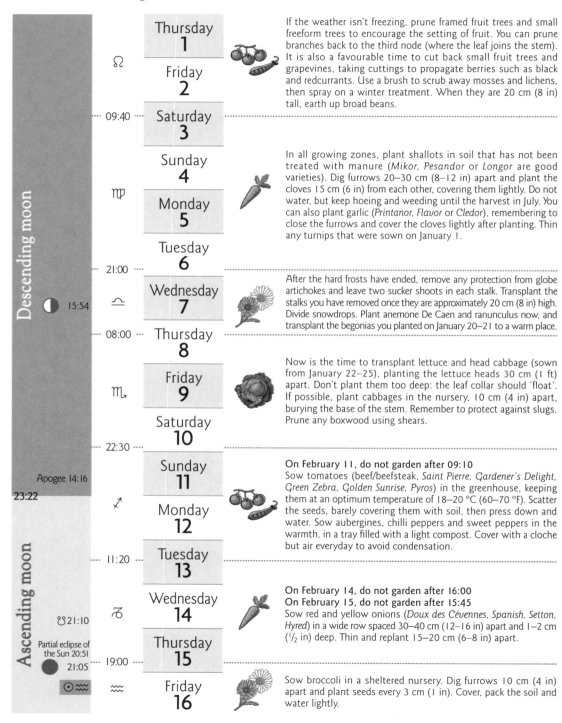

Descending moon

Thursday **1**

Friday **2**

♌

09:40 Saturday **3**

Sunday **4**

♍

Monday **5**

Tuesday **6**

21:00 Wednesday **7**

♎ 15:54

08:00 Thursday **8**

Friday **9**

♏

Saturday **10**

22:30

Ascending moon

Sunday **11**

Apogee 14:16

23:22

♐

Monday **12**

11:20 Tuesday **13**

☊21:10

♑

Wednesday **14**

Partial eclipse of the Sun 20:51

21:05

19:00 Thursday **15**

⊙♒ ♒

Friday **16**

If the weather isn't freezing, prune framed fruit trees and small freeform trees to encourage the setting of fruit. You can prune branches back to the third node (where the leaf joins the stem). It is also a favourable time to cut back small fruit trees and grapevines, taking cuttings to propagate berries such as black and redcurrants. Use a brush to scrub away mosses and lichens, then spray on a winter treatment. When they are 20 cm (8 in) tall, earth up broad beans.

In all growing zones, plant shallots in soil that has not been treated with manure (*Mikor, Pesandor* or *Longor* are good varieties). Dig furrows 20–30 cm (8–12 in) apart and plant the cloves 15 cm (6 in) from each other, covering them lightly. Do not water, but keep hoeing and weeding until the harvest in July. You can also plant garlic (*Printanor, Flavor* or *Cledor*), remembering to close the furrows and cover the cloves lightly after planting. Thin any turnips that were sown on January 1.

After the hard frosts have ended, remove any protection from globe artichokes and leave two sucker shoots in each stalk. Transplant the stalks you have removed once they are approximately 20 cm (8 in) high. Divide snowdrops. Plant anemone De Caen and ranunculus now, and transplant the begonias you planted on January 20–21 to a warm place.

Now is the time to transplant lettuce and head cabbage (sown from January 22–25), planting the lettuce heads 30 cm (1 ft) apart. Don't plant them too deep: the leaf collar should 'float'. If possible, plant cabbages in the nursery, 10 cm (4 in) apart, burying the base of the stem. Remember to protect against slugs. Prune any boxwood using shears.

On February 11, do not garden after 09:10
Sow tomatoes (beef/beefsteak, *Saint Pierre, Gardener's Delight, Green Zebra, Golden Sunrise, Pyros*) in the greenhouse, keeping them at an optimum temperature of 18–20 °C (60–70 °F). Scatter the seeds, barely covering them with soil, then press down and water. Sow aubergines, chilli peppers and sweet peppers in the warmth, in a tray filled with a light compost. Cover with a cloche but air everyday to avoid condensation.

On February 14, do not garden after 16:00
On February 15, do not garden after 15:45
Sow red and yellow onions (*Doux des Cévennes, Spanish, Setton, Hyred*) in a wide row spaced 30–40 cm (12–16 in) apart and 1–2 cm (¹/₂ in) deep. Thin and replant 15–20 cm (6–8 in) apart.

Sow broccoli in a sheltered nursery. Dig furrows 10 cm (4 in) apart and plant seeds every 3 cm (1 in). Cover, pack the soil and water lightly.

Your notes and observations

February 2018

☉ ≈	Friday **16**	Sow summer cauliflowers (*Merveille de toute saisons, Cheddar, Serac*) under shelter or somewhere warm, between 15 °C and 18 °C (60–65 °F). Plant in pots filled with finely sifted compost, tracing small furrows and scattering the seeds. Cover them lightly, tap down and spray with water. Sow Busy Lizzie (impatiens) in pots, leaving uncovered.
≈		
	Saturday **17**	
19:10		
	Sunday **18**	Now, when the Moon is in Pisces, sow Romaine, Batavia or 'cut and come again' lettuce and harvest in May. Sow spring spinach in place (*Palco, Junius, America, Viking*). You can also sow dandelions, cress, rocket (arugula), parsley and chervil at this point, arranging in lines spaced 20–30 cm (8–12 in) apart. Keep damp until they sprout.
♓	Monday **19**	
	Tuesday **20**	
17:20		
♈	Wednesday **21**	Sow round peas, mangetout, sugarsnaps and broad beans. Hoe them when they start growing.
12:00	Thursday **22**	
◑ 08:09	Friday **23**	In a warm place (20–25 °C/70–77 °F), in trays filled with a light compost, sow *Monarch* celeriac. Cover the seeds lightly, pack down and keep damp. In the nursery, sow leeks for summer or autumn harvest (*Pancho, Hannibal*). Thin the young plants after germination, keeping 5 cm (2 in) apart.
♉		
	Saturday **24**	
01:20		
♊	Sunday **25**	Transplant the cauliflowers sown on January 20–21 into individual pots. Prune rose bushes and propagate chrysanthemum and fuchsia from cuttings. Remove any sucker shoots you can find on your globe artichokes.
	Monday **26**	
23:30		
♋	Tuesday **27**	On February 27, do not garden after 09:30 / On February 28, do not garden before 10:10 / Prepare the soil for future asparagus growing. Plant conifers and evergreen shrubs.
10:10	Wednesday **28**	Hoe the peas sown on January 25. Provide supports for climbing varieties.
♌		

Ascending moon

20:12

Descending moon

Perigee 14:39

☊ 05:04

Your notes and observations

March 2018

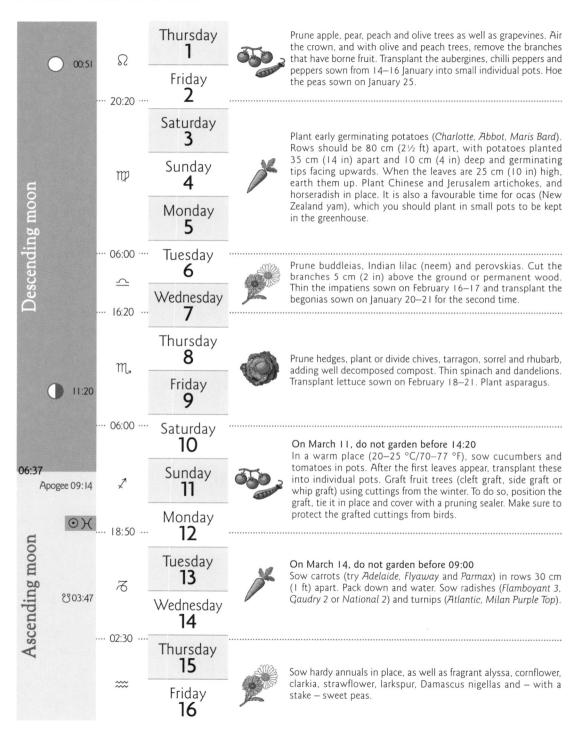

○ 00:51	♌	**Thursday 1**

Prune apple, pear, peach and olive trees as well as grapevines. Air the crown, and with olive and peach trees, remove the branches that have borne fruit. Transplant the aubergines, chilli peppers and peppers sown from 14–16 January into small individual pots. Hoe the peas sown on January 25.

Friday 2
···· 20:20 ····

Saturday 3

♍

Sunday 4

Plant early germinating potatoes (*Charlotte, Abbot, Maris Bard*). Rows should be 80 cm (2½ ft) apart, with potatoes planted 35 cm (14 in) apart and 10 cm (4 in) deep and germinating tips facing upwards. When the leaves are 25 cm (10 in) high, earth them up. Plant Chinese and Jerusalem artichokes, and horseradish in place. It is also a favourable time for ocas (New Zealand yam), which you should plant in small pots to be kept in the greenhouse.

Monday 5

···· 06:00 ····

Tuesday 6

♎

Prune buddleias, Indian lilac (neem) and perovskias. Cut the branches 5 cm (2 in) above the ground or permanent wood. Thin the impatiens sown on February 16–17 and transplant the begonias sown on January 20–21 for the second time.

Wednesday 7

···· 16:20 ····

Thursday 8

♏

Prune hedges, plant or divide chives, tarragon, sorrel and rhubarb, adding well decomposed compost. Thin spinach and dandelions. Transplant lettuce sown on February 18–21. Plant asparagus.

◑ 11:20

Friday 9

···· 06:00 ····

Saturday 10

06:37
Apogee 09:14

♐

On March 11, do not garden before 14:20
In a warm place (20–25 °C/70–77 °F), sow cucumbers and tomatoes in pots. After the first leaves appear, transplant these into individual pots. Graft fruit trees (cleft graft, side graft or whip graft) using cuttings from the winter. To do so, position the graft, tie it in place and cover with a pruning sealer. Make sure to protect the grafted cuttings from birds.

Sunday 11

⊙ ♓

Monday 12

···· 18:50 ····

Tuesday 13

♑

☍ 03:47

On March 14, do not garden before 09:00
Sow carrots (try *Adelaide, Flyaway* and *Parmax*) in rows 30 cm (1 ft) apart. Pack down and water. Sow radishes (*Flamboyant 3, Gaudry 2* or *National 2*) and turnips (*Atlantic, Milan Purple Top*).

Wednesday 14

···· 02:30 ····

Thursday 15

≈

Friday 16

Sow hardy annuals in place, as well as fragrant alyssa, cornflower, clarkia, strawflower, larkspur, Damascus nigellas and – with a stake – sweet peas.

Descending moon

Ascending moon

Your notes and observations

March 2018

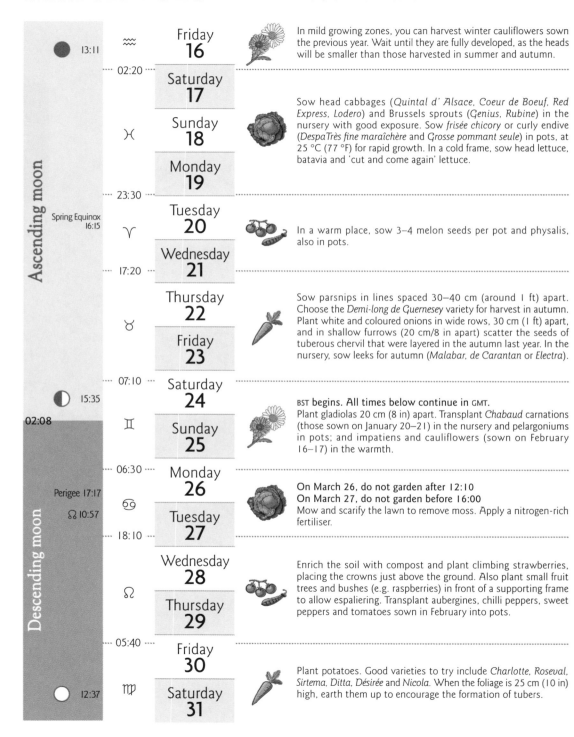

Ascending moon

● 13:11 ≈ **Friday 16**

In mild growing zones, you can harvest winter cauliflowers sown the previous year. Wait until they are fully developed, as the heads will be smaller than those harvested in summer and autumn.

02:20

Saturday 17

✕ **Sunday 18**

Sow head cabbages (*Quintal d' Alsace, Coeur de Boeuf, Red Express, Lodero*) and Brussels sprouts (*Genius, Rubine*) in the nursery with good exposure. Sow *frisée chicory* or curly endive (*DespaTrès fine maraîchère* and *Grosse pommant seule*) in pots, at 25 °C (77 °F) for rapid growth. In a cold frame, sow head lettuce, batavia and 'cut and come again' lettuce.

Monday 19

23:30

Spring Equinox 16:15 ♈ **Tuesday 20**

In a warm place, sow 3–4 melon seeds per pot and physalis, also in pots.

Wednesday 21

17:20

♉ **Thursday 22**

Sow parsnips in lines spaced 30–40 cm (around 1 ft) apart. Choose the *Demi-long de Guernesey* variety for harvest in autumn. Plant white and coloured onions in wide rows, 30 cm (1 ft) apart, and in shallow furrows (20 cm/8 in apart) scatter the seeds of tuberous chervil that were layered in the autumn last year. In the nursery, sow leeks for autumn (*Malabar, de Carantan* or *Electra*).

Friday 23

07:10

◐ 15:35 ♊ **Saturday 24**

BST begins. All times below continue in GMT.
Plant gladiolas 20 cm (8 in) apart. Transplant *Chabaud* carnations (those sown on January 20–21) in the nursery and pelargoniums in pots; and impatiens and cauliflowers (sown on February 16–17) in the warmth.

02:08

Sunday 25

06:30

Perigee 17:17
☊ 10:57 ♋ **Monday 26**

On March 26, do not garden after 12:10
On March 27, do not garden before 16:00
Mow and scarify the lawn to remove moss. Apply a nitrogen-rich fertiliser.

Descending moon

Tuesday 27

18:10

♌ **Wednesday 28**

Enrich the soil with compost and plant climbing strawberries, placing the crowns just above the ground. Also plant small fruit trees and bushes (e.g. raspberries) in front of a supporting frame to allow espaliering. Transplant aubergines, chilli peppers, sweet peppers and tomatoes sown in February into pots.

Thursday 29

05:40

Friday 30

○ 12:37 ♍ **Saturday 31**

Plant potatoes. Good varieties to try include *Charlotte, Roseval, Sirtema, Ditta, Désirée* and *Nicola*. When the foliage is 25 cm (10 in) high, earth them up to encourage the formation of tubers.

Your notes and observations

April 2018

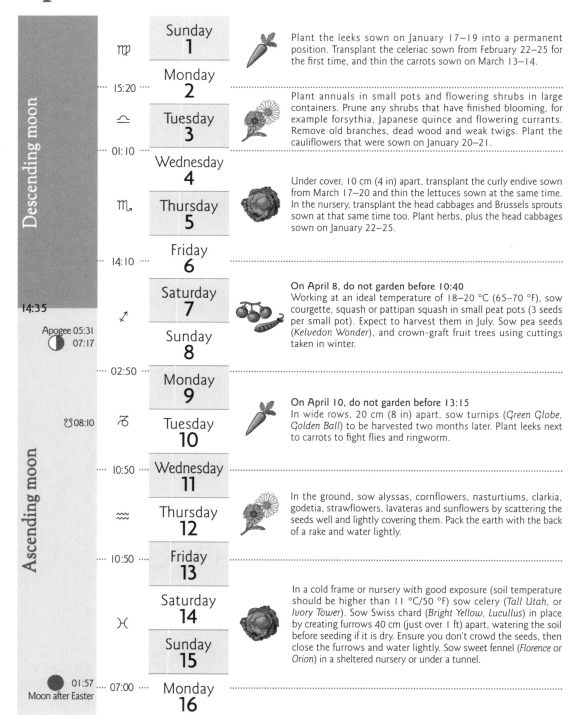

Descending moon

♍	**Sunday 1**	Plant the leeks sown on January 17–19 into a permanent position. Transplant the celeriac sown from February 22–25 for the first time, and thin the carrots sown on March 13–14.
···· 15:20 ····	**Monday 2**	
♎	**Tuesday 3**	Plant annuals in small pots and flowering shrubs in large containers. Prune any shrubs that have finished blooming, for example forsythia, Japanese quince and flowering currants. Remove old branches, dead wood and weak twigs. Plant the cauliflowers that were sown on January 20–21.
···· 01:10 ····	**Wednesday 4**	
♏	**Thursday 5**	Under cover, 10 cm (4 in) apart, transplant the curly endive sown from March 17–20 and thin the lettuces sown at the same time. In the nursery, transplant the head cabbages and Brussels sprouts sown at that same time too. Plant herbs, plus the head cabbages sown on January 22–25.
···· 14:10 ····	**Friday 6**	

14:35

Apogee 05:31
◑ 07:17

Ascending moon

♐	**Saturday 7**	**On April 8, do not garden before 10:40**
	Sunday 8	Working at an ideal temperature of 18–20 °C (65–70 °F), sow courgette, squash or pattipan squash in small peat pots (3 seeds per small pot). Expect to harvest them in July. Sow pea seeds (*Kelvedon Wonder*), and crown-graft fruit trees using cuttings taken in winter.
···· 02:50 ····	**Monday 9**	
☋ 08:10 ♑	**Tuesday 10**	**On April 10, do not garden before 13:15**
		In wide rows, 20 cm (8 in) apart, sow turnips (*Green Globe, Golden Ball*) to be harvested two months later. Plant leeks next to carrots to fight flies and ringworm.
···· 10:50 ····	**Wednesday 11**	
♒	**Thursday 12**	In the ground, sow alyssas, cornflowers, nasturtiums, clarkia, godetia, strawflowers, lavateras and sunflowers by scattering the seeds well and lightly covering them. Pack the earth with the back of a rake and water lightly.
···· 10:50 ····	**Friday 13**	
♓	**Saturday 14**	In a cold frame or nursery with good exposure (soil temperature should be higher than 11 °C/50 °F) sow celery (*Tall Utah*, or *Ivory Tower*). Sow Swiss chard (*Bright Yellow, Lucullus*) in place by creating furrows 40 cm (just over 1 ft) apart, watering the soil before seeding if it is dry. Ensure you don't crowd the seeds, then close the furrows and water lightly. Sow sweet fennel (*Florence* or *Orion*) in a sheltered nursery or under a tunnel.
	Sunday 15	
● 01:57 Moon after Easter ···· 07:00 ····	**Monday 16**	

Your notes and observations

April 2018

Ascending moon

01:57 — Moon after Easter

···· 07:00 ····

Monday 16

♈

Tuesday 17

In mild growing zones, sow three seeds of melon or cucumber in compost.

···· 00:10 ····

Wednesday 18

☉♈

♉

Thursday 19

On April 20, do not garden after 09:35
Sow salsify in the ground, spacing the seeds 20 cm (8 in) apart. Cover the seeds with 2–3 cm (1 in) of fine soil, pack down and water. Keep the soil cool and thin when the plants have 2–3 leaves. Also sow parsnips and parsley root for your winter stock.

Perigee 14:41

···· 12:40 ····

Friday 20

07:39

♊

Saturday 21

In mild zones, plant out the *Semperflorens* begonia, *Chabaud* carnations and pelargoniums that were sown on January 20–21. Plant out the cauliflowers and broccoli sown in February, ensuring they have 70 cm (around 2 ft) in all directions to grow.

···· 12:00 ····

Sunday 22

21:45

♋

☊ 12:20

Monday 23

On April 23, do not garden between 07:15 and 17:25
Under a tunnel, transplant the chicory sown between March 17–20. Protect them from slugs and keep air moving through the tunnel in mild weather. They will be ready for harvest in June–July, after they have been blanched (which takes approximately three weeks).

···· 23:30 ····

Descending moon

Tuesday 24

♌

Wednesday 25

Transplant aubergines, chilli peppers and sweet peppers that were sown January 14–16; tomatoes sown February 11–13; melons sown on March 21; courgette, squash and pattipan squash sown from April 6–8. Delay the planting if the weather is cool. In a warm place, transplant the tomatoes sown March 10–12 and physalis sown on March 21.

···· 12:50 ····

Thursday 26

Friday 27

♍

Saturday 28

In the nursery, do the second transplantation of the celeriac that was sown on February 22–25. Pull out the leeks sown from February 22–25. Dry them for two days on the ground, then replant them. Plant the ocas (New Zealand yam) sown on March 3–5. Thin the parsnips sown on March 22–24, and carrots and turnips sown April 9–11. Hoe and weed between each row.

Sunday 29

···· 23:30 ····

00:58

Monday 30

♎

Plant tuberous begonias, cannas, dahlias, gladiolas and annual flowers. Prune flowering shrubs once the flowers have gone.

Your notes and observations

April

May 2018

In UK/Ireland add 1 hour for BST

Descending moon

Ascending moon

♎ 09:40

Tuesday 1

Thin the hardy annuals that were sown between April 11–13.

♏ **Wednesday 2**

Thursday 3

22:10

Plant aromatic herbs. In your vegetable garden, combine the herbs with vegetables to repel parasites. Mow the lawn. Plant the head cabbage and the Brussels sprouts that were sown between March 17–20, and the sweet fennel sown on April 16.

22:59

Friday 4

♐ **Saturday 5**

On May 6, do not garden before 05:40
Sow broad beans, string beans, green beans and butter beans for shelling. For the smaller varieties, space the rows 40–50 cm (1½ ft) apart, with one seed every 4–5 cm (2 in). For pole beans, sow 5–8 seeds at a time, 40 cm (1 ft) away from the next bunch, in two rows 75 cm (2½ ft) apart. Keep sowing once a month, until the end of July.

Apogee 00:35

10:50

Sunday 6

☋ 10:23

♑ **Monday 7**

◑ 02:08

Tuesday 8

19:20

On May 7, do not garden before 15:30
Sow beets (*Rouge, Crapandine, Kahira*) in wide rows and harvest in the autumn. Sow chicory in rows, lightly covering the seeds. You can also sow leeks for the winter – try the *Bleu de Solaise, de Carentan 2*, or *Saint Victor* varieties.

♒ **Wednesday 9**

Thursday 10

19:50

In the nursery, sow cauliflowers (*Chedder, White Excel*) and broccoli (*Green Magic, Minaret*). Bury the seeds 2 cm (1 in) deep, pack with the back of a rake and water lightly. Harvest in autumn.

Friday 11

♓ **Saturday 12**

Sunday 13

16:30

Sow curly endive in the ground, as well as head and 'cut and come again' lettuce, rocket (arugula) and purslane. Also sow cardoon, chard, coriander (cilantro); and in semi-shade, parsley and chervil. Keep the soil cool. Meanwhile, in the nursery sow Brussels sprouts (*Abacus, Diablo*) and Savoy cabbage (*Protovoy*) for winter and kale varieties (*Reflex* and *Redbor*).

☉♉ ♈ **Monday 14**

09:00

Tuesday 15

Sow courgettes and cucumber in the ground, as well as decorative gourds.

● 11:48

♉ **Wednesday 16**

Sow carrots for winter (try *Chantenay, Parmex, Flyaway* and *Purple Haze*). Scatter the seeds in wide rows, covering lightly, then pack down and water moderately.

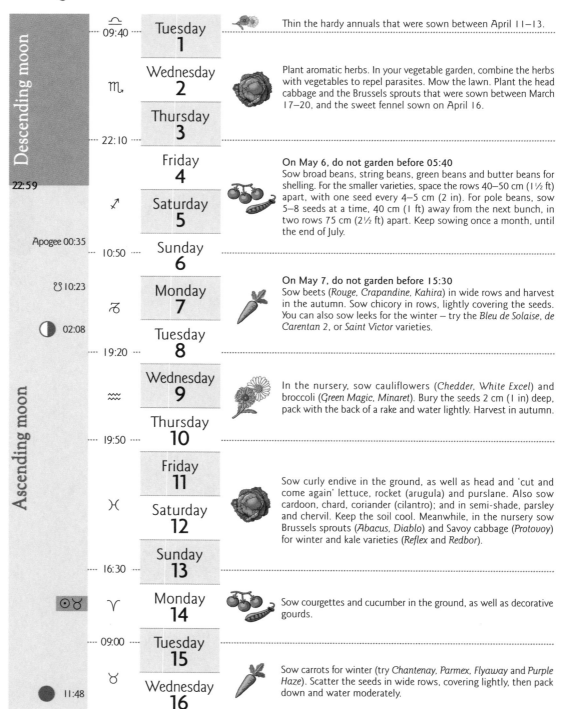

Your notes and observations

May

May 2018

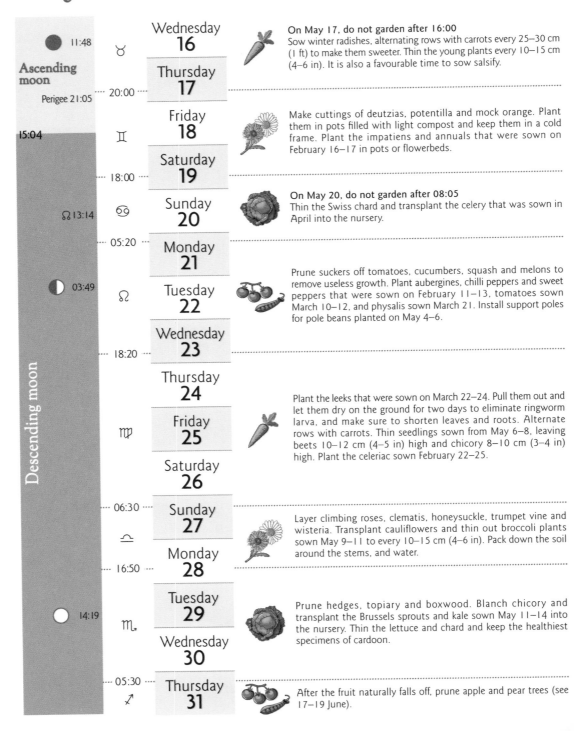

● 11:48

Ascending moon

Perigee 21:05

15:04

♉

--- 20:00 ---

♊

--- 18:00 ---

♋ 13:14

◑ 03:49

♌

--- 18:20 ---

Descending moon

♍

--- 06:30 ---

♎

--- 16:50 ---

○ 14:19

♏

--- 05:30 ---

♐

Wednesday 16

Thursday 17

Friday 18

Saturday 19

Sunday 20

Monday 21

Tuesday 22

Wednesday 23

Thursday 24

Friday 25

Saturday 26

Sunday 27

Monday 28

Tuesday 29

Wednesday 30

Thursday 31

On May 17, do not garden after 16:00
Sow winter radishes, alternating rows with carrots every 25–30 cm (1 ft) to make them sweeter. Thin the young plants every 10–15 cm (4–6 in). It is also a favourable time to sow salsify.

Make cuttings of deutzias, potentilla and mock orange. Plant them in pots filled with light compost and keep them in a cold frame. Plant the impatiens and annuals that were sown on February 16–17 in pots or flowerbeds.

On May 20, do not garden after 08:05
Thin the Swiss chard and transplant the celery that was sown in April into the nursery.

Prune suckers off tomatoes, cucumbers, squash and melons to remove useless growth. Plant aubergines, chilli peppers and sweet peppers that were sown on February 11–13, tomatoes sown March 10–12, and physalis sown March 21. Install support poles for pole beans planted on May 4–6.

Plant the leeks that were sown on March 22–24. Pull them out and let them dry on the ground for two days to eliminate ringworm larva, and make sure to shorten leaves and roots. Alternate rows with carrots. Thin seedlings sown from May 6–8, leaving beets 10–12 cm (4–5 in) high and chicory 8–10 cm (3–4 in) high. Plant the celeriac sown February 22–25.

Layer climbing roses, clematis, honeysuckle, trumpet vine and wisteria. Transplant cauliflowers and thin out broccoli plants sown May 9–11 to every 10–15 cm (4–6 in). Pack down the soil around the stems, and water.

Prune hedges, topiary and boxwood. Blanch chicory and transplant the Brussels sprouts and kale sown May 11–14 into the nursery. Thin the lettuce and chard and keep the healthiest specimens of cardoon.

After the fruit naturally falls off, prune apple and pear trees (see 17–19 June).

Your notes and observations

June 2018

In UK/Ireland add 1 hour for BST

07:08

Apogee 16:34 ···· 18:10 ····

☊ 12:38

Ascending moon

◐ 18:32

02:50

04:10

19:43

00:54 Perigee 23:52

Descending moon

☋ 17:51

♐ Friday **1**

18:10 ···· Saturday **2**

♑ Sunday **3**

Monday **4**

02:50 ···· Tuesday **5**

≈ Wednesday **6**

04:10 ···· Thursday **7**

♓ Friday **8**

Saturday **9**

02:20 ···· Sunday **10**

♈ Monday **11**

19:10 ···· Tuesday **12**

♉ Wednesday **13**

05:30 ···· Thursday **14**

♊ Friday **15**

02:20 ···· Saturday **16**

♋

On June 2, do not garden after 11:30
Sow beans such as *Phenomene, Abundance, Minidor, Argus* and *Contender*. At the end of the row, sow nasturtiums to attract aphids. Sow sweetcorn in bunches of 4 or 5 seeds, spaced 50 cm (2 ft) apart. Thin out the corn after it starts growing.

On June 3, do not garden between 07:30 and 17:45
Sow chicory in rows 30 cm (1 ft) apart, try varieties such as *Indigo, Witloof de Brussels* and *Zuckerhut*. Re-seed carrots (*Chantenay, Purple Haze*).

Pick flowers for teas and dry in a dark, clean, well-ventilated room. In the nursery, sow biennials (for example, campanula, wallflower, forget-me-not, Sweet William and primula) and perennials (oriental poppy, hollyhock).

If the weather is dry, use the middle of the day to cut aromatic herbs before they bloom (tarragon, bay (laurel), mint, rosemary, sage and thyme), as well as nettles and comfrey (to make manure tea). Let them dry before use. In rows 30 cm (1 ft) apart, sow escarole, wild chicory and radicchio (*Indigo* and *Red Treviso*), and re-seed lettuces using heat-hardy varieties such as *Iceberg, Baby gem,* or *Kinemontpas*.

Sow cucumbers and courgettes (zucchini) in patches, and beans in rows.

Sow winter radishes (*China Rose, Black radish* and *Violet de Gournay*) and swedes (rutabaga) in rows 30–40 cm (1 ft) apart. Re-seed parsnips and carrots to harvest from autumn to the beginning of winter, scattering seeds in furrows and covering lightly with fine soil. Pack down and water lightly.

On June 15, do not garden before 05:00
Layer wisteria and trumpet vine. Divide hyacinths, daffodils (narcissus), and tulips when the leaves turn yellow. Plant the broccoli that was sown on May 9–11.

On June 16, do not garden after 12:45
Plant the celery that was sown on April 14–16.

Your notes and observations

June 2018

In UK/Ireland add 1 hour for BST

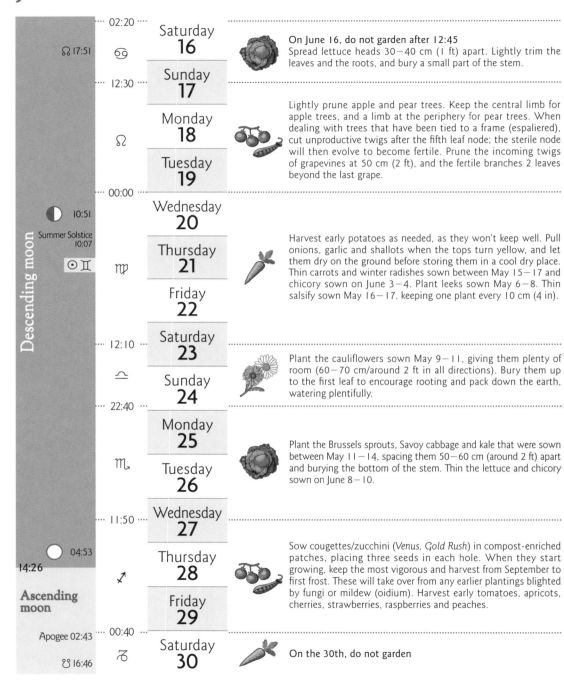

Descending moon

♌ 17:51

02:20 — ♋ — Saturday 16, Sunday 17

On June 16, do not garden after 12:45
Spread lettuce heads 30–40 cm (1 ft) apart. Lightly trim the leaves and the roots, and bury a small part of the stem.

12:30 — ♌ — Sunday 17, Monday 18, Tuesday 19

Lightly prune apple and pear trees. Keep the central limb for apple trees, and a limb at the periphery for pear trees. When dealing with trees that have been tied to a frame (espaliered), cut unproductive twigs after the fifth leaf node; the sterile node will then evolve to become fertile. Prune the incoming twigs of grapevines at 50 cm (2 ft), and the fertile branches 2 leaves beyond the last grape.

00:00 — ♍ — Wednesday 20, Thursday 21, Friday 22, Saturday 23

◐ 10:51

Summer Solstice 10:07

☉ ♊

Harvest early potatoes as needed, as they won't keep well. Pull onions, garlic and shallots when the tops turn yellow, and let them dry on the ground before storing them in a cool dry place. Thin carrots and winter radishes sown between May 15–17 and chicory sown on June 3–4. Plant leeks sown May 6–8. Thin salsify sown May 16–17, keeping one plant every 10 cm (4 in).

12:10 — ♎ — Saturday 23, Sunday 24

Plant the cauliflowers sown May 9–11, giving them plenty of room (60–70 cm/around 2 ft in all directions). Bury them up to the first leaf to encourage rooting and pack down the earth, watering plentifully.

22:40 — ♏ — Monday 25, Tuesday 26, Wednesday 27

Plant the Brussels sprouts, Savoy cabbage and kale that were sown between May 11–14, spacing them 50–60 cm (around 2 ft) apart and burying the bottom of the stem. Thin the lettuce and chicory sown on June 8–10.

11:50 — ♐ — Wednesday 27, Thursday 28, Friday 29

○ 04:53

14:26

Ascending moon

Sow cougettes/zucchini (*Venus, Gold Rush*) in compost-enriched patches, placing three seeds in each hole. When they start growing, keep the most vigorous and harvest from September to first frost. These will take over from any earlier plantings blighted by fungi or mildew (oidium). Harvest early tomatoes, apricots, cherries, strawberries, raspberries and peaches.

00:40 — ♑ — Saturday 30

Apogee 02:43

☋ 16:46

On the 30th, do not garden

Your notes and observations

July 2018

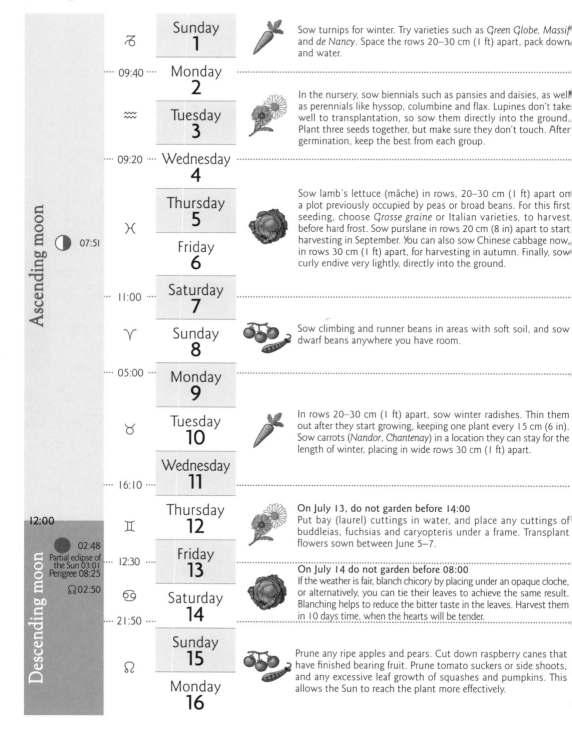

Ascending moon

♐   Sunday **1**

Sow turnips for winter. Try varieties such as *Green Globe*, *Massif* and *de Nancy*. Space the rows 20–30 cm (1 ft) apart, pack down and water.

···· 09:40 ····   Monday **2**

≈   Tuesday **3**

In the nursery, sow biennials such as pansies and daisies, as well as perennials like hyssop, columbine and flax. Lupines don't take well to transplantation, so sow them directly into the ground. Plant three seeds together, but make sure they don't touch. After germination, keep the best from each group.

···· 09:20 ····   Wednesday **4**

Thursday **5**

♓   ◑ 07:51

Friday **6**

Sow lamb's lettuce (mâche) in rows, 20–30 cm (1 ft) apart on a plot previously occupied by peas or broad beans. For this first seeding, choose *Grosse graine* or Italian varieties, to harvest before hard frost. Sow purslane in rows 20 cm (8 in) apart to start harvesting in September. You can also sow Chinese cabbage now, in rows 30 cm (1 ft) apart, for harvesting in autumn. Finally, sow curly endive very lightly, directly into the ground.

··· 11:00 ···   Saturday **7**

♈   Sunday **8**

Sow climbing and runner beans in areas with soft soil, and sow dwarf beans anywhere you have room.

··· 05:00 ···   Monday **9**

♉   Tuesday **10**

In rows 20–30 cm (1 ft) apart, sow winter radishes. Thin them out after they start growing, keeping one plant every 15 cm (6 in). Sow carrots (*Nandor*, *Chantenay*) in a location they can stay for the length of winter, placing in wide rows 30 cm (1 ft) apart.

Wednesday **11**

··· 16:10 ···

Descending moon

12:00

● 02:48
Partial eclipse of
the Sun 03:01
Perigree 08:25

♌ 02:50

♊   Thursday **12**

On July 13, do not garden before 14:00
Put bay (laurel) cuttings in water, and place any cuttings of buddleias, fuchsias and caryopteris under a frame. Transplant flowers sown between June 5–7.

··· 12:30 ···   Friday **13**

On July 14 do not garden before 08:00
If the weather is fair, blanch chicory by placing under an opaque cloche, or alternatively, you can tie their leaves to achieve the same result. Blanching helps to reduce the bitter taste in the leaves. Harvest them in 10 days time, when the hearts will be tender.

♋   Saturday **14**

··· 21:50 ···

♌   Sunday **15**

Prune any ripe apples and pears. Cut down raspberry canes that have finished bearing fruit. Prune tomato suckers or side shoots, and any excessive leaf growth of squashes and pumpkins. This allows the Sun to reach the plant more effectively.

Monday **16**

Your notes and observations

July

July 2018

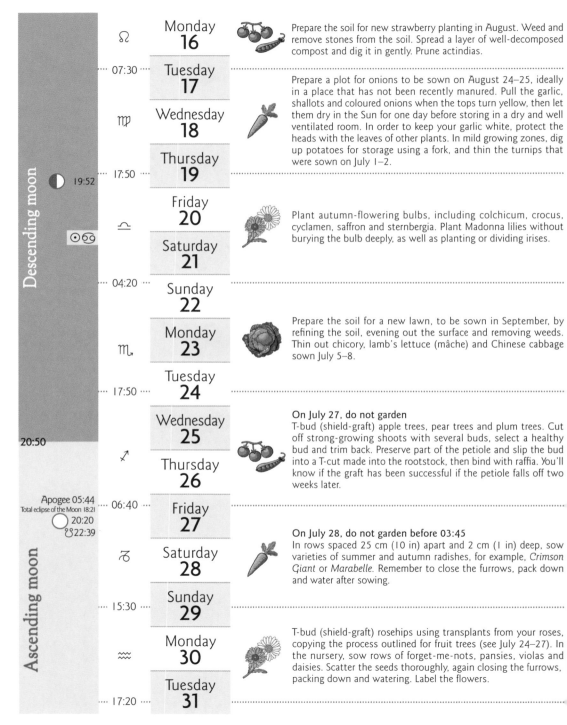

Descending moon

♌

Monday
16

Prepare the soil for new strawberry planting in August. Weed and remove stones from the soil. Spread a layer of well-decomposed compost and dig it in gently. Prune actindias.

···· 07:30 ····

Tuesday
17

Prepare a plot for onions to be sown on August 24–25, ideally in a place that has not been recently manured. Pull the garlic, shallots and coloured onions when the tops turn yellow, then let them dry in the Sun for one day before storing in a dry and well ventilated room. In order to keep your garlic white, protect the heads with the leaves of other plants. In mild growing zones, dig up potatoes for storage using a fork, and thin the turnips that were sown on July 1–2.

♍

Wednesday
18

Thursday
19

···· 17:50 ····

◐ 19:52

Friday
20

Plant autumn-flowering bulbs, including colchicum, crocus, cyclamen, saffron and sternbergia. Plant Madonna lilies without burying the bulb deeply, as well as planting or dividing irises.

♎

⊙♋

Saturday
21

···· 04:20 ····

Sunday
22

Monday
23

Prepare the soil for a new lawn, to be sown in September, by refining the soil, evening out the surface and removing weeds. Thin out chicory, lamb's lettuce (mâche) and Chinese cabbage sown July 5–8.

♏

Tuesday
24

···· 17:50 ····

20:50

Wednesday
25

On July 27, do not garden
T-bud (shield-graft) apple trees, pear trees and plum trees. Cut off strong-growing shoots with several buds, select a healthy bud and trim back. Preserve part of the petiole and slip the bud into a T-cut made into the rootstock, then bind with raffia. You'll know if the graft has been successful if the petiole falls off two weeks later.

♐

Thursday
26

Apogee 05:44
Total eclipse of the Moon 18:21
○ 20:20
☋22:39

···· 06:40 ····

Friday
27

On July 28, do not garden before 03:45
In rows spaced 25 cm (10 in) apart and 2 cm (1 in) deep, sow varieties of summer and autumn radishes, for example, *Crimson Giant* or *Marabelle*. Remember to close the furrows, pack down and water after sowing.

Ascending moon

♑

Saturday
28

···· 15:30 ····

Sunday
29

Monday
30

T-bud (shield-graft) rosehips using transplants from your roses, copying the process outlined for fruit trees (see July 24–27). In the nursery, sow rows of forget-me-nots, pansies, violas and daisies. Scatter the seeds thoroughly, again closing the furrows, packing down and watering. Label the flowers.

♒

Tuesday
31

···· 17:20 ····

Your notes and observations

August 2018

In UK/Ireland add 1 hour for BST

Ascending moon

Wednesday 1

Thursday 2 ♓

Sow weather-hardy lamb's lettuce (mâche) varieties, such as *Coquille de Louvier*, *Verte de Cambrai* and *Vit*, as well as Chinese cabbage (*Granaat*, *Yuki* and *bok-choy*). Sow spinach (*Perpetual*, *America* or *Palco*) in rows 20 – 30 cm (1 ft) apart. You can also sow 'cut and come again' lettuce to harvest before the hard cold sets in, for example *Red Salad Bowl* and *Grenadine*, or sow winter varieties to harvest in spring.

···· 17:50 ····
Friday 3

Saturday 4 ♈

Harvest shelling beans, to eat fresh or for drying.

☽ 18:18

···· 13:10 ····
Sunday 5

Monday 6 ♉

Sow winter radishes (*China Rose*, *Black Spanish*) and turnips (*Armand*, *Purple Top*, *Milan*) in place. Plant in rows 20 cm (8 in) apart, and keep them cool until harvesting. You could also sow leeks, at the same spacing, scattering the seeds well. When they start growing, thin them out to 5 cm (2 in) apart, keeping the healthiest plants. To be harvested in May 2019.

Tuesday 7

···· 02:10 ····
Wednesday 8

22:30

Thursday 9 ♊

Prune roses, cutting the stalks to approximately 15 cm (6 in) long. Remove basil leaves and plant the cuttings in a light compost. Transplant any flowers that were sown July 2–4. Be sure to give them 10 cm (4 in) in all directions for growth.

···· 00:30 ····
Friday 10 ♋

☋ 13:40
Perigee 18:07
☉☋ Partial eclipse of the Sun 09:46
09:58

On August 10, do not garden after 08:35
On August 11, do not garden before 15:00
Prune deciduous hedges, topiary and boxwood. Clear fallow areas.

···· 08:30 ····
Saturday 11

Descending moon

Sunday 12 ♌

Plant strawberries. Dampen the clods, remove them from pots and place the bare roots into holes enriched with compost. Do not bury the collar. Pack down and water. After the harvest, prune peach trees and apricot trees beyond the two twigs at the bottom, which will bear fruit next year.

Monday 13

···· 17:10 ····
Tuesday 14

Wednesday 15 ♍

Pull beets, celeriac, carrots, turnips and autumn radishes as you need them. Consume them promptly to get the most out of their many vitamins and minerals. Dig up potatoes, onions, shallots and garlic. Store them in a well-ventilated room, and in the case of potatoes, away from the light.

Thursday 16

Your notes and observations

August 2018

In UK/Ireland add I hour for BST

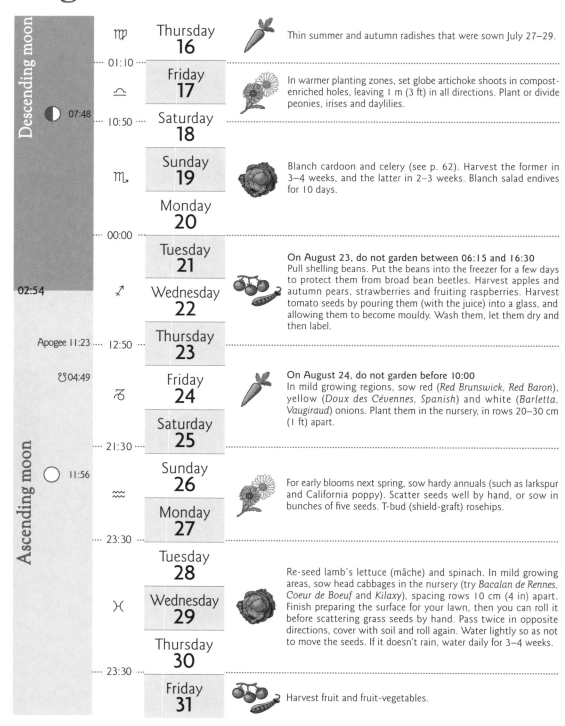

Descending moon

♍ Thursday **16**

Thin summer and autumn radishes that were sown July 27–29.

···· 01:10 ····

♎ Friday **17**

In warmer planting zones, set globe artichoke shoots in compost-enriched holes, leaving 1 m (3 ft) in all directions. Plant or divide peonies, irises and daylilies.

···· 10:50 ····

Saturday **18**

♏ Sunday **19**

Blanch cardoon and celery (see p. 62). Harvest the former in 3–4 weeks, and the latter in 2–3 weeks. Blanch salad endives for 10 days.

Monday **20**

···· 00:00 ····

Tuesday **21**

♐ Wednesday **22**

On August 23, do not garden between 06:15 and 16:30
Pull shelling beans. Put the beans into the freezer for a few days to protect them from broad bean beetles. Harvest apples and autumn pears, strawberries and fruiting raspberries. Harvest tomato seeds by pouring them (with the juice) into a glass, and allowing them to become mouldy. Wash them, let them dry and then label.

Apogee 11:23 ···· 12:50 ····

Thursday **23**

☊04:49

♑ Friday **24**

On August 24, do not garden before 10:00
In mild growing regions, sow red (*Red Brunswick, Red Baron*), yellow (*Doux des Cévennes, Spanish*) and white (*Barletta, Vaugiraud*) onions. Plant them in the nursery, in rows 20–30 cm (1 ft) apart.

Saturday **25**

···· 21:30 ····

Ascending moon

○ 11:56

♒ Sunday **26**

For early blooms next spring, sow hardy annuals (such as larkspur and California poppy). Scatter seeds well by hand, or sow in bunches of five seeds. T-bud (shield-graft) rosehips.

Monday **27**

···· 23:30 ····

Tuesday **28**

♓ Wednesday **29**

Re-seed lamb's lettuce (mâche) and spinach. In mild growing areas, sow head cabbages in the nursery (try *Bacalan de Rennes, Coeur de Boeuf* and *Kilaxy*), spacing rows 10 cm (4 in) apart. Finish preparing the surface for your lawn, then you can roll it before scattering grass seeds by hand. Pass twice in opposite directions, cover with soil and roll again. Water lightly so as not to move the seeds. If it doesn't rain, water daily for 3–4 weeks.

Thursday **30**

···· 23:30 ····

Friday **31**

Harvest fruit and fruit-vegetables.

02:54

07:48

Your notes and observations

September 2018 In UK/Ireland add 1 hour for BST

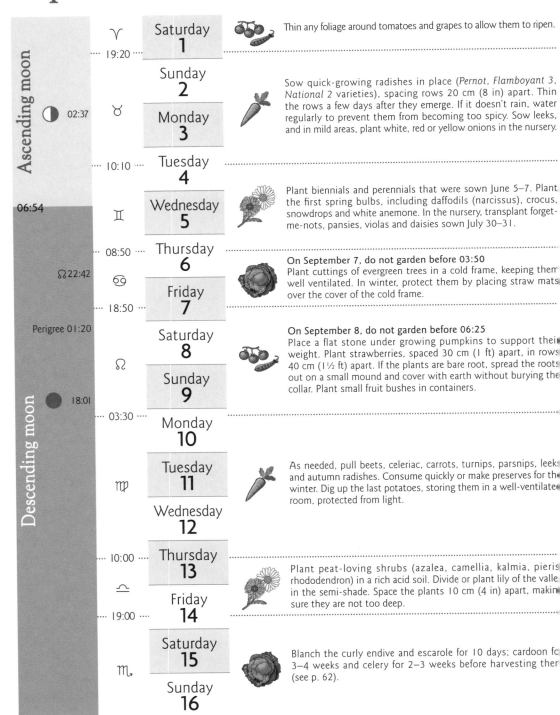

Ascending moon

♈
···· 19:20 ····
◐ 02:37 ♉
···· 10:10 ····
06:54 ♊
☊ 22:42 ♋
···· 08:50 ····
···· 18:50 ····
Perigree 01:20 ♌
● 18:01
···· 03:30 ····

Descending moon

♍
···· 10:00 ····
♎
···· 19:00 ····
♏

Saturday 1	Thin any foliage around tomatoes and grapes to allow them to ripen.
Sunday 2 / **Monday 3**	Sow quick-growing radishes in place (*Pernot, Flamboyant 3, National 2* varieties), spacing rows 20 cm (8 in) apart. Thin the rows a few days after they emerge. If it doesn't rain, water regularly to prevent them from becoming too spicy. Sow leeks, and in mild areas, plant white, red or yellow onions in the nursery.
Tuesday 4 / **Wednesday 5**	Plant biennials and perennials that were sown June 5–7. Plant the first spring bulbs, including daffodils (narcissus), crocus, snowdrops and white anemone. In the nursery, transplant forget-me-nots, pansies, violas and daisies sown July 30–31.
Thursday 6 / **Friday 7**	On September 7, do not garden before 03:50 Plant cuttings of evergreen trees in a cold frame, keeping them well ventilated. In winter, protect them by placing straw mats over the cover of the cold frame.
Saturday 8 / **Sunday 9**	On September 8, do not garden before 06:25 Place a flat stone under growing pumpkins to support their weight. Plant strawberries, spaced 30 cm (1 ft) apart, in rows 40 cm (1½ ft) apart. If the plants are bare root, spread the roots out on a small mound and cover with earth without burying the collar. Plant small fruit bushes in containers.
Monday 10	
Tuesday 11 / **Wednesday 12**	As needed, pull beets, celeriac, carrots, turnips, parsnips, leeks and autumn radishes. Consume quickly or make preserves for the winter. Dig up the last potatoes, storing them in a well-ventilated room, protected from light.
Thursday 13 / **Friday 14**	Plant peat-loving shrubs (azalea, camellia, kalmia, pieris, rhododendron) in a rich acid soil. Divide or plant lily of the valley in the semi-shade. Space the plants 10 cm (4 in) apart, making sure they are not too deep.
Saturday 15 / **Sunday 16**	Blanch the curly endive and escarole for 10 days; cardoon for 3–4 weeks and celery for 2–3 weeks before harvesting them (see p. 62).

Your notes and observations

September 2018 In UK/Ireland add 1 hour for BST

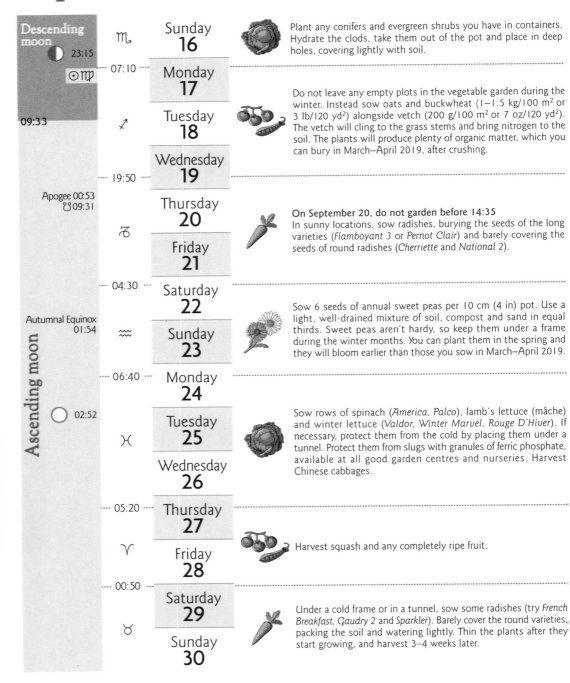

Descending moon
◑ 23:15
09:33

Apogee 00:53
℧ 09:31

Autumnal Equinox
01:54

Ascending moon

○ 02:52

♏
07:10 ⊙ ♍
♐
19:50

♑

04:30
♒

06:40
♓

05:20
♈

00:50
♉

Sunday **16**	Plant any conifers and evergreen shrubs you have in containers. Hydrate the clods, take them out of the pot and place in deep holes, covering lightly with soil.
Monday **17**	
Tuesday **18**	Do not leave any empty plots in the vegetable garden during the winter. Instead sow oats and buckwheat (1–1.5 kg/100 m² or 3 lb/120 yd²) alongside vetch (200 g/100 m² or 7 oz/120 yd²). The vetch will cling to the grass stems and bring nitrogen to the soil. The plants will produce plenty of organic matter, which you can bury in March–April 2019, after crushing.
Wednesday **19**	
Thursday **20**	**On September 20, do not garden before 14:35** In sunny locations, sow radishes, burying the seeds of the long varieties (*Flamboyant 3* or *Pernot Clair*) and barely covering the seeds of round radishes (*Cherriette* and *National 2*).
Friday **21**	
Saturday **22**	Sow 6 seeds of annual sweet peas per 10 cm (4 in) pot. Use a light, well-drained mixture of soil, compost and sand in equal thirds. Sweet peas aren't hardy, so keep them under a frame during the winter months. You can plant them in the spring and they will bloom earlier than those you sow in March–April 2019.
Sunday **23**	
Monday **24**	Sow rows of spinach (*America, Palco*), lamb's lettuce (*mâche*) and winter lettuce (*Valdor, Winter Marvel, Rouge D'Hiver*). If necessary, protect them from the cold by placing them under a tunnel. Protect them from slugs with granules of ferric phosphate, available at all good garden centres and nurseries. Harvest Chinese cabbages.
Tuesday **25**	
Wednesday **26**	
Thursday **27**	Harvest squash and any completely ripe fruit.
Friday **28**	
Saturday **29**	Under a cold frame or in a tunnel, sow some radishes (try *French Breakfast, Gaudry 2* and *Sparkler*). Barely cover the round varieties, packing the soil and watering lightly. Thin the plants after they start growing, and harvest 3–4 weeks later.
Sunday **30**	

Your notes and observations

October 2018

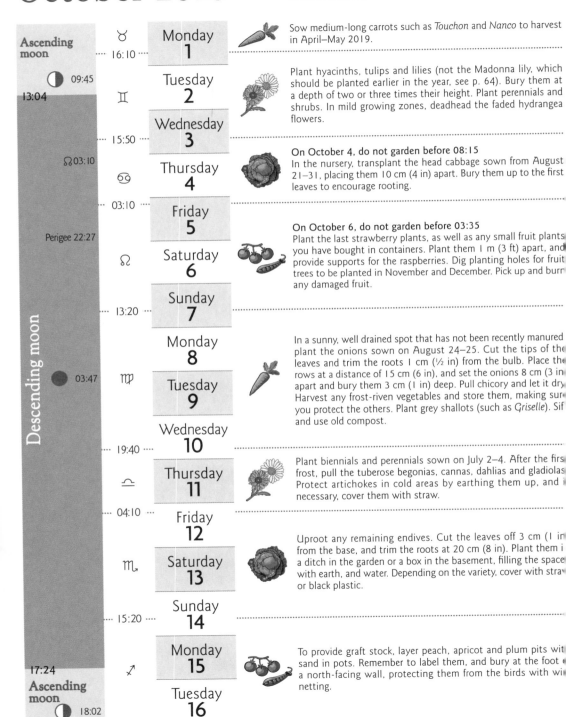

Ascending moon

◐ 09:45

13:04

♉ 16:10

Monday 1

Sow medium-long carrots such as *Touchon* and *Nanco* to harvest in April–May 2019.

Tuesday 2

♊

Wednesday 3

15:50

Plant hyacinths, tulips and lilies (not the Madonna lily, which should be planted earlier in the year, see p. 64). Bury them at a depth of two or three times their height. Plant perennials and shrubs. In mild growing zones, deadhead the faded hydrangea flowers.

☊ 03:10

♋

Thursday 4

On October 4, do not garden before 08:15
In the nursery, transplant the head cabbage sown from August 21–31, placing them 10 cm (4 in) apart. Bury them up to the first leaves to encourage rooting.

03:10

Friday 5

Perigee 22:27

♌

Saturday 6

On October 6, do not garden before 03:35
Plant the last strawberry plants, as well as any small fruit plants you have bought in containers. Plant them 1 m (3 ft) apart, and provide supports for the raspberries. Dig planting holes for fruit trees to be planted in November and December. Pick up and burn any damaged fruit.

13:20

Sunday 7

Descending moon

● 03:47

♍

Monday 8

In a sunny, well drained spot that has not been recently manured, plant the onions sown on August 24–25. Cut the tips of the leaves and trim the roots 1 cm (½ in) from the bulb. Place the rows at a distance of 15 cm (6 in), and set the onions 8 cm (3 in) apart and bury them 3 cm (1 in) deep. Pull chicory and let it dry. Harvest any frost-riven vegetables and store them, making sure you protect the others. Plant grey shallots (such as *Griselle*). Sift and use old compost.

Tuesday 9

Wednesday 10

19:40

♎

Thursday 11

Plant biennials and perennials sown on July 2–4. After the first frost, pull the tuberose begonias, cannas, dahlias and gladiolas. Protect artichokes in cold areas by earthing them up, and if necessary, cover them with straw.

04:10

Friday 12

♏

Saturday 13

Uproot any remaining endives. Cut the leaves off 3 cm (1 in) from the base, and trim the roots at 20 cm (8 in). Plant them in a ditch in the garden or a box in the basement, filling the space with earth, and water. Depending on the variety, cover with straw or black plastic.

15:20

Sunday 14

17:24

♐

Ascending moon

◑ 18:02

Monday 15

To provide graft stock, layer peach, apricot and plum pits with sand in pots. Remember to label them, and bury at the foot of a north-facing wall, protecting them from the birds with wire netting.

Tuesday 16

Your notes and observations

October 2018

In UK/Ireland add 1 hour for BST

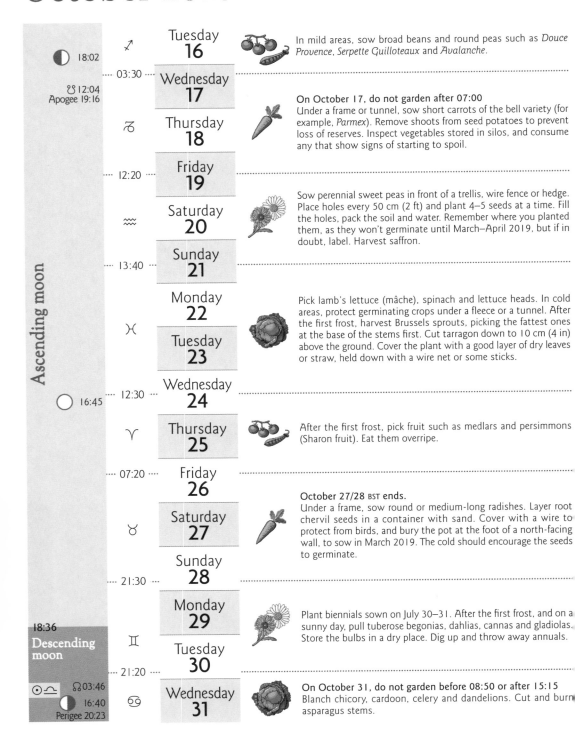

◐ 18:02	♐	**Tuesday 16**

In mild areas, sow broad beans and round peas such as *Douce Provence*, *Serpette Guilloteaux* and *Avalanche*.

···· 03:30 ····

Wednesday 17

☊ 12:04
Apogee 19:16

♑

Thursday 18

On October 17, do not garden after 07:00
Under a frame or tunnel, sow short carrots of the bell variety (for example, *Parmex*). Remove shoots from seed potatoes to prevent loss of reserves. Inspect vegetables stored in silos, and consume any that show signs of starting to spoil.

···· 12:20 ····

Friday 19

♒

Saturday 20

Sow perennial sweet peas in front of a trellis, wire fence or hedge. Place holes every 50 cm (2 ft) and plant 4–5 seeds at a time. Fill the holes, pack the soil and water. Remember where you planted them, as they won't germinate until March–April 2019, but if in doubt, label. Harvest saffron.

···· 13:40 ····

Sunday 21

Monday 22

♓

Tuesday 23

Pick lamb's lettuce (mâche), spinach and lettuce heads. In cold areas, protect germinating crops under a fleece or a tunnel. After the first frost, harvest Brussels sprouts, picking the fattest ones at the base of the stems first. Cut tarragon down to 10 cm (4 in) above the ground. Cover the plant with a good layer of dry leaves or straw, held down with a wire net or some sticks.

○ 16:45 ···· 12:30 ····

Wednesday 24

♈

Thursday 25

After the first frost, pick fruit such as medlars and persimmons (Sharon fruit). Eat them overripe.

···· 07:20 ····

Friday 26

♉

Saturday 27

October 27/28 BST ends.
Under a frame, sow round or medium-long radishes. Layer root chervil seeds in a container with sand. Cover with a wire to protect from birds, and bury the pot at the foot of a north-facing wall, to sow in March 2019. The cold should encourage the seeds to germinate.

···· 21:30 ····

Sunday 28

Ascending moon

Monday 29

♊

Tuesday 30

Plant biennials sown on July 30–31. After the first frost, and on a sunny day, pull tuberose begonias, dahlias, cannas and gladiolas. Store the bulbs in a dry place. Dig up and throw away annuals.

···· 21:20 ····

18:36
Descending moon

☉♎ ☋03:46
◐ 16:40
Perigee 20:23

♋

Wednesday 31

On October 31, do not garden before 08:50 or after 15:15
Blanch chicory, cardoon, celery and dandelions. Cut and burn asparagus stems.

Your notes and observations

November 2018

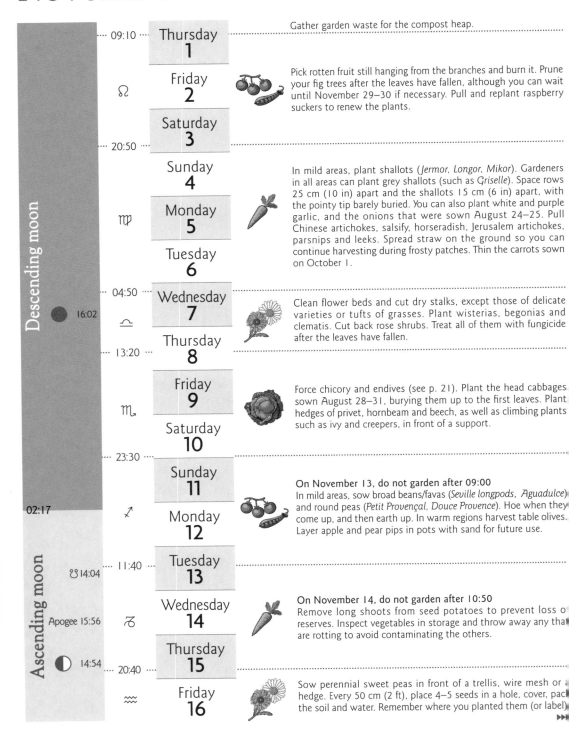

Time	Day	Sign	Notes
09:10	**Thursday 1**		Gather garden waste for the compost heap.
	Friday 2	♌	Pick rotten fruit still hanging from the branches and burn it. Prune your fig trees after the leaves have fallen, although you can wait until November 29–30 if necessary. Pull and replant raspberry suckers to renew the plants.
20:50	**Saturday 3**		
	Sunday 4		In mild areas, plant shallots (*Jermor, Longor, Mikor*). Gardeners in all areas can plant grey shallots (such as *Griselle*). Space rows 25 cm (10 in) apart and the shallots 15 cm (6 in) apart, with the pointy tip barely buried. You can also plant white and purple garlic, and the onions that were sown August 24–25. Pull Chinese artichokes, salsify, horseradish, Jerusalem artichokes, parsnips and leeks. Spread straw on the ground so you can continue harvesting during frosty patches. Thin the carrots sown on October 1.
	Monday 5	♍	
	Tuesday 6		
04:50	**Wednesday 7**	♎	Clean flower beds and cut dry stalks, except those of delicate varieties or tufts of grasses. Plant wisterias, begonias and clematis. Cut back rose shrubs. Treat all of them with fungicide after the leaves have fallen.
13:20	**Thursday 8**		
	Friday 9	♏	Force chicory and endives (see p. 21). Plant the head cabbages sown August 28–31, burying them up to the first leaves. Plant hedges of privet, hornbeam and beech, as well as climbing plants such as ivy and creepers, in front of a support.
23:30	**Saturday 10**		
	Sunday 11		On November 13, do not garden after 09:00
	Monday 12	♐	In mild areas, sow broad beans/favas (*Seville longpods, Aguadulce*) and round peas (*Petit Provençal, Douce Provence*). Hoe when they come up, and then earth up. In warm regions harvest table olives. Layer apple and pear pips in pots with sand for future use.
11:40	**Tuesday 13**		
	Wednesday 14	♑	On November 14, do not garden after 10:50
20:40	**Thursday 15**		Remove long shoots from seed potatoes to prevent loss of reserves. Inspect vegetables in storage and throw away any that are rotting to avoid contaminating the others.
	Friday 16	♒	Sow perennial sweet peas in front of a trellis, wire mesh or a hedge. Every 50 cm (2 ft), place 4–5 seeds in a hole, cover, pack the soil and water. Remember where you planted them (or label).

Descending moon

16:02

02:17

Ascending moon

☋ 14:04

Apogee 15:56

14:54

Your notes and observations

November 2018

Ascending moon

Descending moon

≈

22:30

Friday
16

Saturday
17

as they won't germinate until March–April 2019. Care for any flowering plants you have in the house by placing a layer of clay marbles in a saucer, adding 2–3 cm (1 in) of water and putting the pots on top. The air around the plant will be more humid, but the roots won't rot.

♓

Sunday
18

Monday
19

Harvest Brussels sprouts, lamb's lettuce (mâche), spinach and lettuce. Protect the most fragile from the cold. In a sprouting jar or cup, germinate lentils, chickpeas or soybeans. The delicious young shoots are rich in vitamins and minerals. In a pot in the warmth sow orange, lemon or kumquat seeds to grow pretty, exotic-looking plants.

♏ 21:40

Tuesday
20

Wednesday
21

♈

In mild areas, sow round peas and mangetout.

16:00

Thursday
22

○ 05:39

Friday
23

♉

Saturday
24

Under a frame, sow a few round radishes (*Amethyst*, *Gaudry 2*) and some short, bell-shaped carrots (*Parmex*). A few days after they emerge, thin them, saving one plant every 5 cm (2 in). Protect from slugs but air them for brief periods in milder weather.

04:40

Sunday
25

01:50

Perigee 12:12

♊

Monday
26

On November 26, do not garden after 07:05
If there's no frost, plant roses and flowering shrubs with bare roots. If grafting your roses, remember to secure the join with grafting tape. Reinforce protection for delicate crops such as globe artichokes.

☊05:17

03:20

Tuesday
27

♋

On November 27, do not garden before 10:25
Prune hazelnuts and any existing older bamboo canes (3–5 year old) that can be used as stakes for future gardening. Force chicory and endives (see p. 21).

14:30

Wednesday
28

◑ 00:19

♌

Thursday
29

Friday
30

Prune fruit trees and brush the trunks to remove moss and lichens. Enrich the surrounding soil with compost and slow release fertiliser. If it isn't freezing, plant more bare-root trees without burying the grafts.

Your notes and observations

December 2018

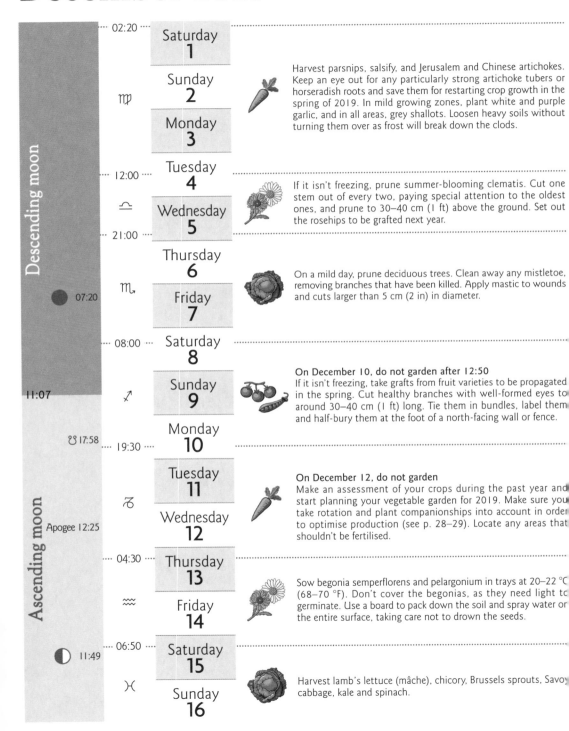

Descending moon

02:20 — Saturday **1**

♍ — Sunday **2**

Monday **3**

12:00 — Tuesday **4**

♎ — Wednesday **5**

21:00

Thursday **6**

♏ — Friday **7**

● 07:20

08:00 — Saturday **8**

11:07

♐ — Sunday **9**

☽ 17:58 — 19:30 — Monday **10**

Ascending moon

♑ — Tuesday **11**

Apogee 12:25 — Wednesday **12**

04:30 — Thursday **13**

♒ — Friday **14**

◐ 11:49 — 06:50 — Saturday **15**

♓ — Sunday **16**

Harvest parsnips, salsify, and Jerusalem and Chinese artichokes. Keep an eye out for any particularly strong artichoke tubers or horseradish roots and save them for restarting crop growth in the spring of 2019. In mild growing zones, plant white and purple garlic, and in all areas, grey shallots. Loosen heavy soils without turning them over as frost will break down the clods.

If it isn't freezing, prune summer-blooming clematis. Cut one stem out of every two, paying special attention to the oldest ones, and prune to 30–40 cm (1 ft) above the ground. Set out the rosehips to be grafted next year.

On a mild day, prune deciduous trees. Clean away any mistletoe, removing branches that have been killed. Apply mastic to wounds and cuts larger than 5 cm (2 in) in diameter.

On December 10, do not garden after 12:50
If it isn't freezing, take grafts from fruit varieties to be propagated in the spring. Cut healthy branches with well-formed eyes to around 30–40 cm (1 ft) long. Tie them in bundles, label them and half-bury them at the foot of a north-facing wall or fence.

On December 12, do not garden
Make an assessment of your crops during the past year and start planning your vegetable garden for 2019. Make sure you take rotation and plant companionships into account in order to optimise production (see p. 28–29). Locate any areas that shouldn't be fertilised.

Sow begonia semperflorens and pelargonium in trays at 20–22 °C (68–70 °F). Don't cover the begonias, as they need light to germinate. Use a board to pack down the soil and spray water on the entire surface, taking care not to drown the seeds.

Harvest lamb's lettuce (mâche), chicory, Brussels sprouts, Savoy cabbage, kale and spinach.

Your notes and observations

December

December 2018

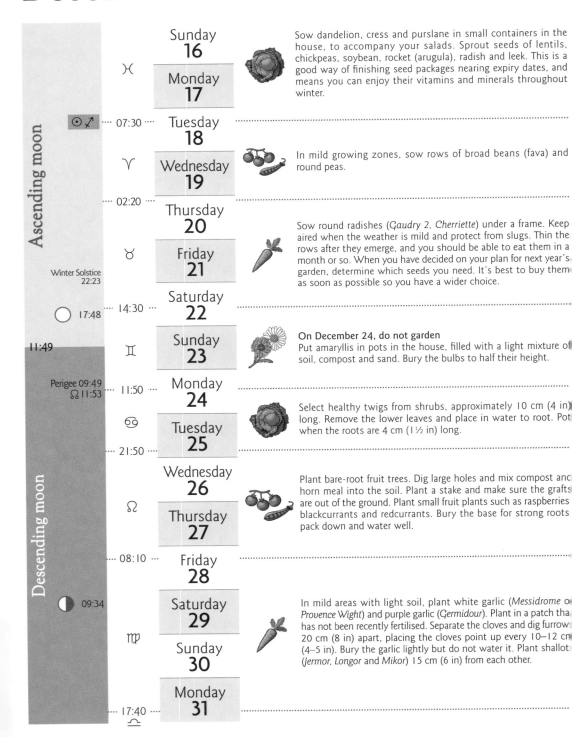

⊙♐ 07:30

Winter Solstice
22:23

○ 17:48 14:30

11:49

Perigee 09:49
☊ 11:53 11:50

21:50

◐ 09:34

08:10

17:40

♓
♈
♉
♊
♋
♌
♍
♎

02:20

Sunday
16

Monday
17

Tuesday
18

Wednesday
19

Thursday
20

Friday
21

Saturday
22

Sunday
23

Monday
24

Tuesday
25

Wednesday
26

Thursday
27

Friday
28

Saturday
29

Sunday
30

Monday
31

Sow dandelion, cress and purslane in small containers in the house, to accompany your salads. Sprout seeds of lentils, chickpeas, soybean, rocket (arugula), radish and leek. This is a good way of finishing seed packages nearing expiry dates, and means you can enjoy their vitamins and minerals throughout winter.

In mild growing zones, sow rows of broad beans (fava) and round peas.

Sow round radishes (*Gaudry 2*, *Cherriette*) under a frame. Keep aired when the weather is mild and protect from slugs. Thin the rows after they emerge, and you should be able to eat them in a month or so. When you have decided on your plan for next year's garden, determine which seeds you need. It's best to buy them as soon as possible so you have a wider choice.

On December 24, do not garden
Put amaryllis in pots in the house, filled with a light mixture of soil, compost and sand. Bury the bulbs to half their height.

Select healthy twigs from shrubs, approximately 10 cm (4 in) long. Remove the lower leaves and place in water to root. Pot when the roots are 4 cm (1½ in) long.

Plant bare-root fruit trees. Dig large holes and mix compost and horn meal into the soil. Plant a stake and make sure the grafts are out of the ground. Plant small fruit plants such as raspberries blackcurrants and redcurrants. Bury the base for strong roots pack down and water well.

In mild areas with light soil, plant white garlic (*Messidrome* o *Provence Wight*) and purple garlic (*Germidour*). Plant in a patch tha has not been recently fertilised. Separate the cloves and dig furrow 20 cm (8 in) apart, placing the cloves point up every 10–12 cm (4–5 in). Bury the garlic lightly but do not water it. Plant shallot (*Jermor*, *Longor* and *Mikor*) 15 cm (6 in) from each other.

Your notes and observations

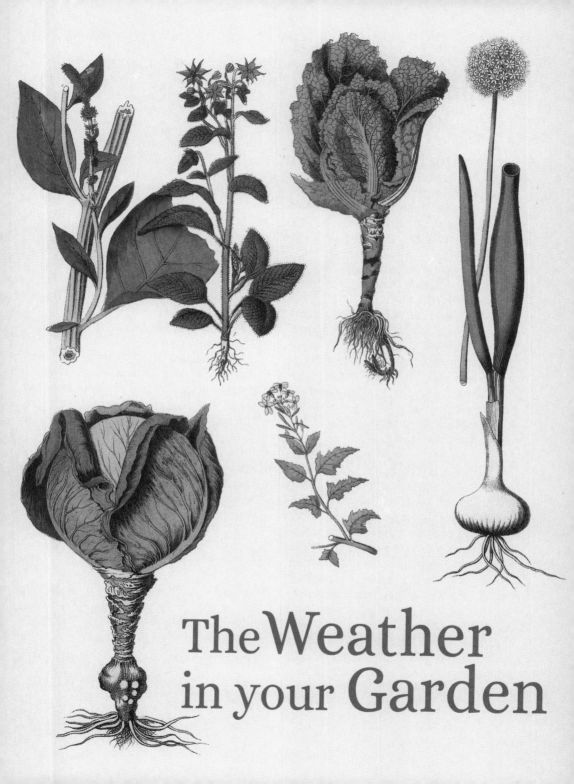

The Weather
in your Garden

Your Weather Journal

Observing the weather

You will often notice differences between the weather forecast and the actual weather in your garden. There are several ways to better predict the weather where you live, but here we will look at the simplest and most natural.

It also helps to record details about the weather in a logbook and on the monthly charts provided here (pp. 92–103). The more specific your notes are, the more accurate your predictions will become. In turn, you will take greater pleasure in observing nature and the movements of the sky. A logbook is a very useful tool for recording your gardening experience. You can carry it over from year to year, enriching your knowledge and easing the planning of seasonal and daily tasks.

What to look for

Altitude and other features of the local landscape can affect the weather in your garden: there may be a hill or mountain nearby, or perhaps a tree, hedge or wall protects you from the wind. The reverse may be true: a valley might channel important air currents, or a nearby lake may create an updraught. Microclimates are infinite and your garden is unique, which means so are its weather patterns.

Will it be warm and sunny? Will it rain? It can help to look at the sky for clues. A bright moon surrounded by a halo, or a veiled sun in the evening often mean rain.

Through observation, you can learn which wind drives away clouds, clears the sky or allows the Sun to shine. Birds and insects can 'smell' the rain or an approaching thunderstorm, behaving in ways we can recognise and use too. The shape of the clouds can also help; consult an illustrated book on clouds for reference.

Soli-lunar charts

How to use them

The soli-lunar charts shown here are graduated in 5° bands with 0° marking the equator. Positive declinations are above the equator line and negative declinations below. If you are in the Southern hemisphere, turn the chart upside down.

- Dates of the lunar phases, Moon nodes, perigees and apogees are all marked and a key to symbols used is provided on p.36
- The path of the Sun is marked in dark green, and the Moon in light green
- As in the example on p.90, make notes every day, for example the colour of the sky, any rain, sun, clear weather, variable wind, the lowest night temperature, highest daytime temperature, etc.

The Sun

On January 1 at midnight (00:00), the declination[1] of the Sun is −23°03´ (see chart p. 92). The Sun is gaining height from its lowest point at the winter solstice.

At the time of the spring equinox, the curve of the Sun intersects with the equator and day and night are the same duration. The Sun's declination becomes positive, temperatures gradually climb, sap rises in plants and flowers start to bloom.

The Sun reaches its highest point (+23°26´) at the time of the summer solstice on June 21, before starting its descent, crossing the equator again at the time of the autumn equinox (p. 100) and falling to its lowest level at the winter solstice (23°26´, p. 103).

The constant pace of the Sun, identical every year, regulates the length of our days, and the rise and fall of plants' sap.

The Moon

The Moon's movement, changes from one year to the next in relation to the Earth, the Sun and the ecliptic, thus causing many variations.

In 2018, the Moon is in ascendance on the first day of the year, arriving at its highest lunistice[2] as it enters Gemini, on January 1 at 23:58. It then descends, crossing the Equator on January 8 to reach its lowest lunistice on January 15 at 16:30, in Sagittarius.

There are 13 days, 15 hours, 15 minutes and 30 seconds between two lunistices and the crossings of the equator, the complete cycle of the sidereal revolution being 27 days, 7 hours, 43 minutes and 11 seconds.

Changes in weather usually occur at the time of lunistices, especially on the third day.

Let's take an example in April

Note carefully the weather on April 7, 8, and 9 in particular.

- If the weather is fair and the wind blows from the direction of the good weather, it should last until the full moon on the 16th.
- If the weather is variable on the 9th, and changeable with cloudy skies, you can expect sunny intervals ahead. Note that on the day the Moon crosses the equator (14th) there may be some small changes.

Remember, when it comes to weather forecasting, no system is infallible. Hopefully, this method will help you to plan your gardening tasks in some way.

---

1 Declination: distance of a star from the plane of the celestial equator (horizontal line 0° on the charts).
2 Lunistice: time when the Moon reaches the farthest angular distance north or south of the celestial equator.

Soli-lunar Charts

How to use the charts: an example

Each monthly chart allows you to note the main weather variations each day.

	Rain (mm) daily	Rain (mm) month to date	Temperature (°C) min	Temperature (°C) max	Wind	Air pressure	Weather features
31 Tue			5	10	SE		Fair sunny intervals, mild
30 Mon	3	62	4	7		1042	Overcast, drizzle, mild
29 Sun			−2	7		1045	Fog, rain, sunny intervals
28 Sat	10	59	2	6		1040	Light showers, fog in the evening
27 Fri			5	3	SE	1036	Cloudy
26 Thu			−6	2	SE	1036	Overcast, wind gusts in the evening
25 Wed			−8	4		1042	Sunny intervals
24 Tue			−8	4	N	1043	Fair
23 Mon			−3	6		1042	Fair to cloudy
22 Sun Ap.			−4	7		1044	Overcast
21 Sat			−6	8		1045	Fair
20 Fri			−7	3		1046	Fair
19 Thu			−11	3		1046	Fair, milder
18 Wed			−11	−1		1045	Sunny, cold
17 Tue			−7	1	NE	1041	Fair, cold
16 Mon	2	49	−2	2	N	1042	Some snow in the morning, sunny intervals
15 Sun	3	47	−3	1		1043	Snow in the morning, some sun
14 Sat	22	44	−4	1		1042	Snow turning to rain
13 Fri	4	22	−1	5		1039	Snow early and for the rest of the day
12 Thu	5	18	2	6		1032	Fog, rain
11 Wed	13		−2	5		1045	Fog, rain
10 Tue Per.			1	5	NO	1036	Fog, overcast
9 Mon			−6	3		1044	Sunny intervals
8 Sun			−4	4		1050	Fair
7 Sat			−7	5		1051	Fair
6 Fri			−8	1		1053	Fair, some clouds
5 Thu			−4	3	NO	1051	Fair
4 Wed			−8	2		1045	Fair, milder
3 Tue			−6	3	NO	1047	Fair, then cold
2 Mon			−5	5		1045	Sunny intervals, light clouds
1 Sun			−3	5		1044	Fair

This example was noted in January 2017. The third day after the lunistice, January 13 and 27 provide important indications for the 10 days following.

90

+30° +25° +20° +15° +10° +5° 0° −5° −10° −15° −20° −25° −30°

In dark green, the passage of the Sun in front of Sagittarius and Capricorn. In light green, the curve and passage of the Moon in front of the constellations.

This chart allows you to visualise the large curve of the Sun, the small monthly curves of the Moon, their ascending movement (times for sowing) and descending movement (times for preparing the earth, transplanting and planting).

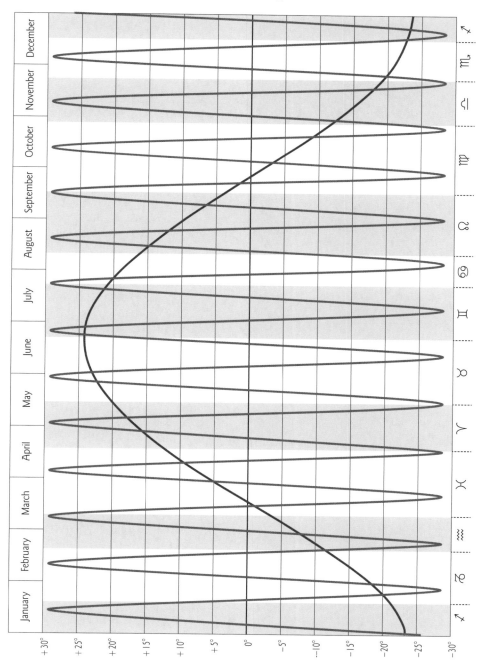

January 2018

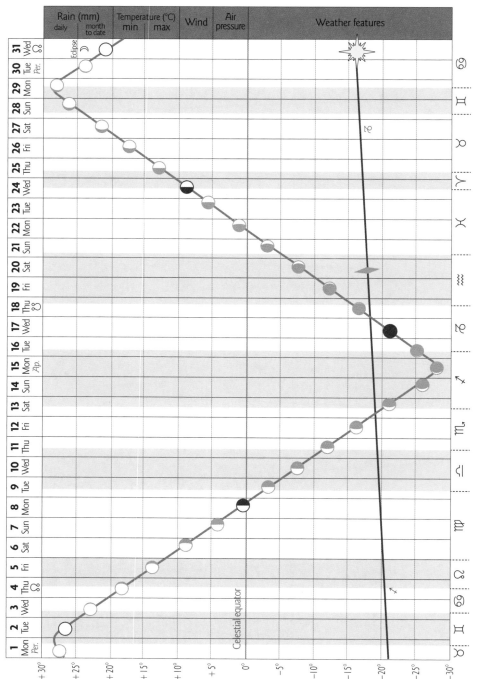

In dark green: the passage of the Sun in front of Sagittarius and Capricorn. In light green: the curve and passage of the Moon in front of the constellations.

February 2018

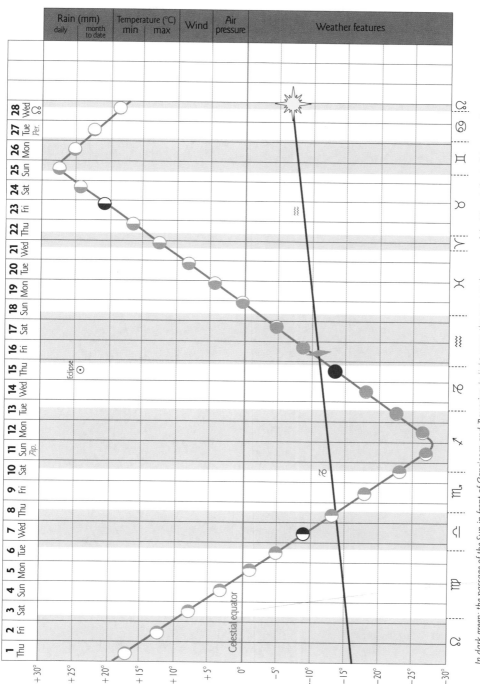

| | Rain (mm) | | Temperature (°C) | | Wind | Air | Weather features |
| | daily | month to date | min | max | | pressure | |

In dark green: the passage of the Sun in front of Capricorn and Aquarius. In light green: the curve and passage of the Moon in front of the constellations.

March 2018

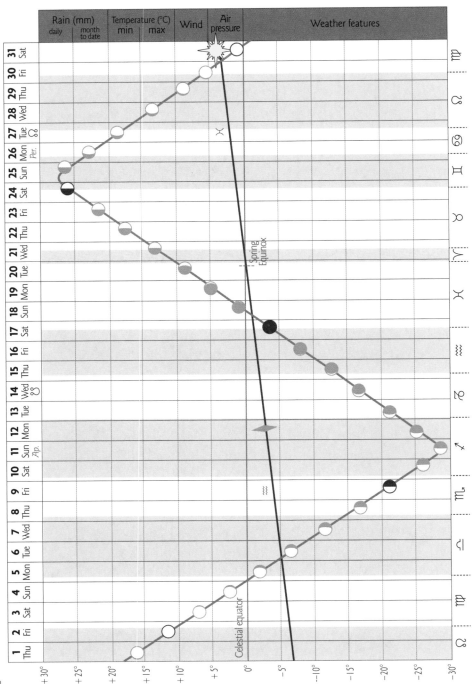

	Rain (mm)		Temperature (°C)		Wind	Air pressure	Weather features
	daily	month to date	min	max			

In dark green: the passage of the Sun in front of Aquarius and Pisces. In light green: the curve and passage of the Moon in front of the constellations.

April 2018

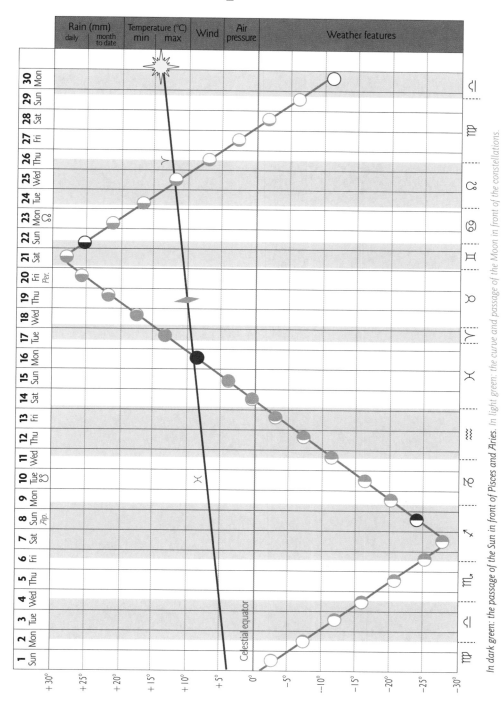

In dark green: the passage of the Sun in front of Pisces and Aries. In light green: the curve and passage of the Moon in front of the constellations.

May 2018

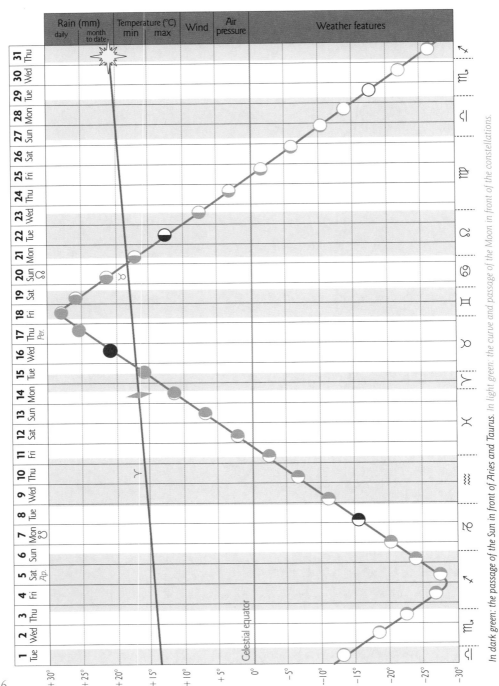

Rain (mm) daily / month to date	Temperature (°C) min / max	Wind	Air pressure	Weather features

In dark green: the passage of the Sun in front of Aries and Taurus. In light green: the curve and passage of the Moon in front of the constellations.

June 2018

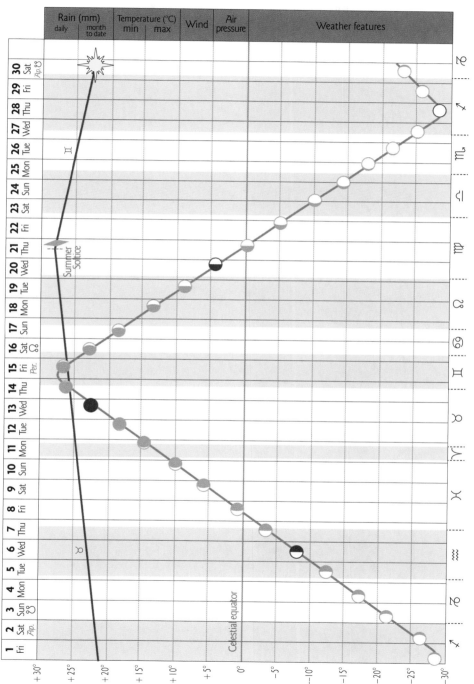

Rain (mm)		Temperature (°C)		Wind	Air pressure	Weather features
daily	month to date	min	max			

In dark green: the passage of the Sun in front of Taurus and Gemini. In light green: the curve and passage of the Moon in front of the constellations.

July 2018

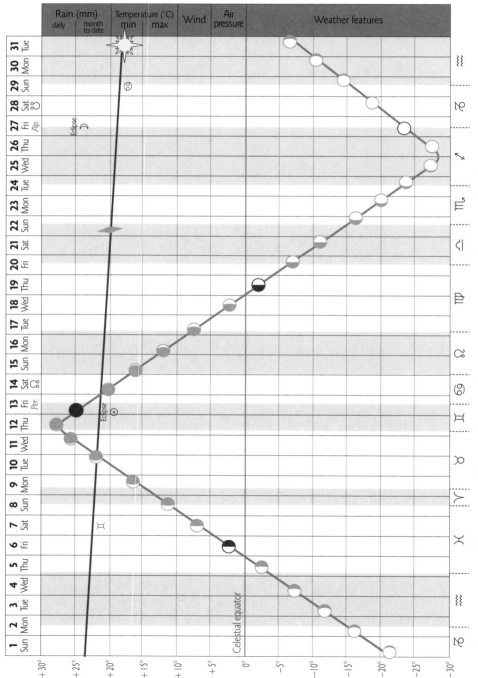

Rain (mm)		Temperature (°C)		Wind	Air pressure	Weather features
daily	month to date	min	max			

In dark green: the passage of the Sun in front of Gemini and Cancer. In light green: the curve and passage of the Moon in front of the constellations.

98

August 2018

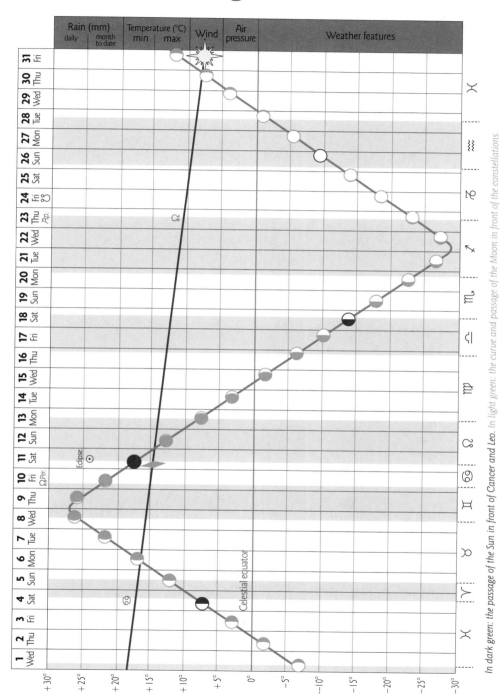

In dark green: the passage of the Sun in front of Cancer and Leo. In light green: the curve and passage of the Moon in front of the constellations.

September 2018

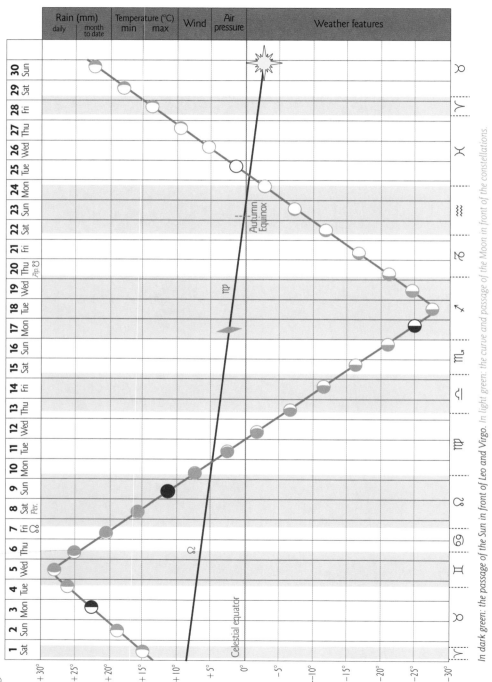

Rain (mm)		Temperature (°C)		Wind	Air pressure	Weather features
daily	month to date	min	max			

In dark green: the passage of the Sun in front of Leo and Virgo. In light green: the curve and passage of the Moon in front of the constellations.

Autumn Equinox

Celestial equator

October 2018

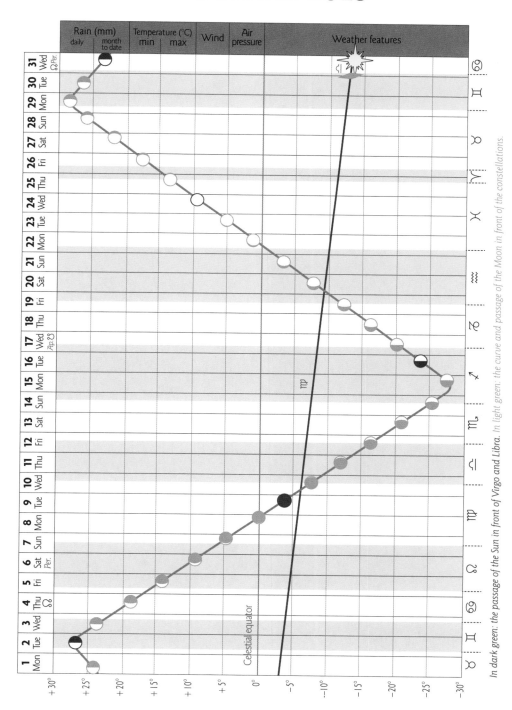

In dark green: the passage of the Sun in front of Virgo and Libra. In light green: the curve and passage of the Moon in front of the constellations.

November 2018

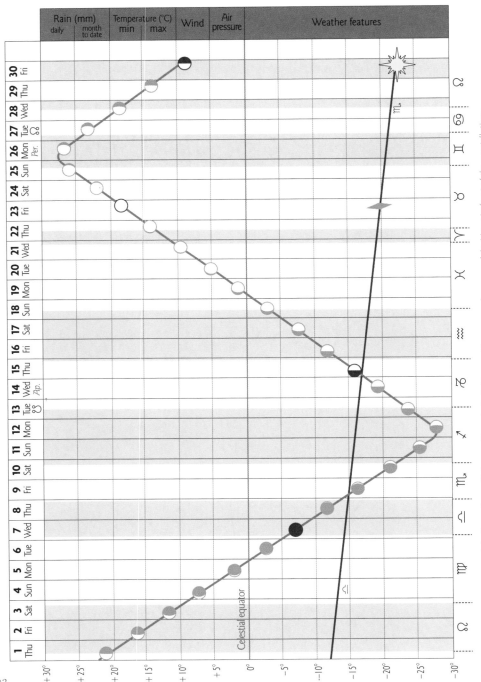

Rain (mm)		Temperature (°C)		Wind	Air pressure	Weather features
daily	month to date	min	max			

In dark green: the passage of the Sun in front of Libra and Scorpio. In light green: the curve and passage of the Moon in front of the constellations.

December 2018

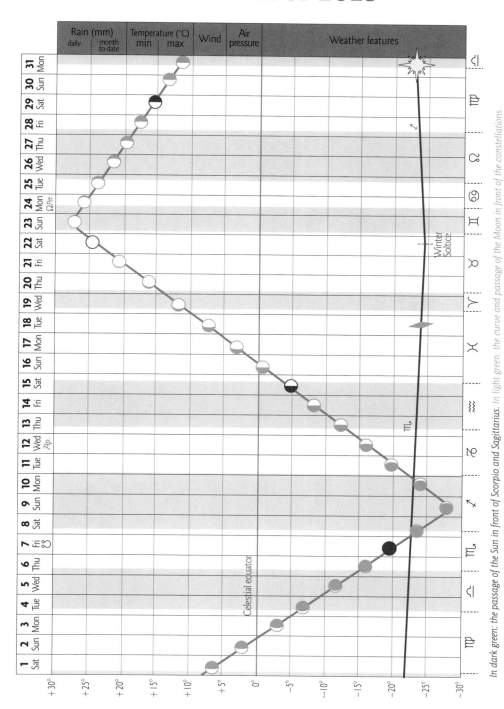

	Rain (mm)		Temperature (°C)		Wind	Air pressure	Weather features
	daily	month to date	min	max			

Celestial ecuator

Winter Solstice

In dark green: the passage of the Sun in front of Scorpio and Sagittarius. In light green: the curve and passage of the Moon in front of the constellations.

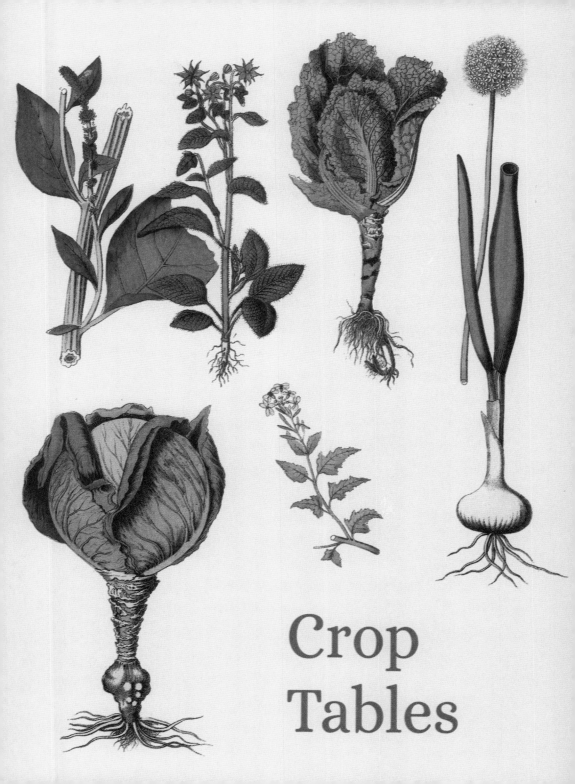

Crop
Tables

Annual crop tables

These annual crop tables will give you the best dates for sowing, planting and pruning according to the Moon. It is up to you to decide your personal gardening methods, and whether to grow your crops somewhere sheltered or on open ground, depending on the climate of your garden. The calendar pages (pp. 38–85) give all the necessary details about the Moon's cycles, but you can use them with the crop tables to keep track of which tasks you should do on a particular day by looking for the highlighted dates. Suggested soil temperatures stated on the tables are for sowing in the open earth (unless otherwise specified), but note that soil temperatures need to be higher for early seeding in containers. As mentioned earlier, it may be that you can't always follow our indicated harvest dates. On these days, we would suggest you make use of time indoors and do some garden planning, or perhaps make preserves with any crops you have already grown and harvested.

In the Vegetable Garden

Flowering vegetables

- Sow and plant in the greenhouse, under cover or in the open, depending on the season and the climate of your garden
- Sow with the ascendant moon in Aquarius ≈≈
- Plant, hoe and earth up with the descending moon in Gemini ♊ or Libra ♎

	Jan	Feb	Mar	Apr	May	Jun	Jul	Aug	Sep	Oct	Nov	Dec
Artichoke (globe)												
→ Remove earth. Keep two suckers from each stem		7/26	6/25	3/30				9/17	14			
→ Plant			6/25	3/30				9/17	14	3/11/30		
→ Water, fertilise, hoe			6/25	3/30	1/18/27	15/24	21	9/17	14			
→ Harvest					9	6	3.30	26	23			
→ Turn down, cover										3/11/30	7	4
Broccoli												
→ Sow (soil at 15 °C/60 °F*)		16	15	12	9	6	3/30					
→ Water gently, transplant, hoe			6/25	3/30	1/18/27	15/24	21	9/17	14	3/11/30		
→ Harvest			15	12	9	6	3/30	26	23	20	16	
Cauliflower												
→ Sow (soil at 15 °C/60 °F*)	20	16	15	12	9	6						
→ Water regularly, transplant, hoe		7/26	6/25	3/30	1/18/27	15/24	21	9/17	14	3/11/30		
→ Harvest			15	12	9	6	3/30	26	23	20	16	

The cultivation of the vegetable is explained in the Calendar on the highlighted date.

*Ideal soil temperature for good germination.

Leafy vegetables

- Sow and plant in the greenhouse, under cover or in the open depending on the season and the climate of your garden
- Sow with the ascendant moon in Pisces ♓
- Plant, hoe and earth up with the descending moon in Cancer ♋ or Scorpio ♏

	Jan	Feb	Mar	Apr	May	Jun	Jul	Aug	Sep	Oct	Nov	Dec
Asparagus												
→ Prepare and enrich the soil	3/13	9								13	9	
→ Plant 1–2 year old crowns			8	5								
→ Hoe			8	5								
→ Harvest the older plants				14	12							
→ Cut, burn, add compost										13	9	
Cardoon												
→ Prepare and enrich the soil			8	5						13	9	
→ Sow (soil at 10 °C/50 °F*)					12							
→ Thin plants, hoe, water					29	26	23	19	7/16			
→ Earth up, blanch								19	7/16	13	9	
→ Harvest									25	22	19	16
Celery												
→ Prepare and enrich the soil		9	8									
→ Sow (soil at 12 °C/53 °F*)			18	14	12							
→ Transplant, hoe				5	2/29	26	23	19	7/16			
→ Earth up, blanch								23	19	7/16	13	9
→ Harvest								2/29	25	22	19	16
Chicory												
→ Transplant, force, blanch	3/13									13/31	9/27	6/25
Fennel												
→ Prepare and enrich the soil			8									
→ Sow (soil at 12 °C/53 °F*)				14	12	8	5	2/29				
→ Thin out, hoe					2/29	26	23	19	7/16			
→ Harvest							5	2/29	25	22	19	16
Spinach												
→ Prepare and enrich the soil	3/13	9					23	19	7/16	13	9	
→ Sow (soil at 12 °C/53 °F*)		19	18	14				2/29	25			
→ Thin out, hoe			8	5	2/29			19	7/16	13	9	
→ Harvest	22	19	18	14	12	8				22	19	16
Swiss chard												
→ Prepare and enrich the soil			8							13	9	
→ Sow (soil at 10 °C/50 °F*)				14	12	8						
→ Thin, hoe					2/29	26	23	19	7/16	13		
→ Harvest			18	14	12		5	2/29	25	22	19	

The cultivation of the vegetable is explained in the Calendar on the highlighted date.

*Ideal soil temperature for good germination.

Year-round cabbages

- Sow and plant in the greenhouse, under cover or in the open depending on the season and the climate of your garden
- Sow with the ascendant moon in Pisces ♓
- Plant, hoe and earth up with the descending moon in Cancer ♋ or Scorpio ♏

	Jan	Feb	Mar	Apr	May	Jun	Jul	Aug	Sep	Oct	Nov	Dec
Brussels sprouts												
Prepare and enrich soil		9	8	5						13	9	
Sow in nursery			18	14	12							
Transplant in nursery, maintain				5	2/29	26						
Plant, maintain				5	2/29	26	23	19	7/16	13		
Harvest	22	19	18						25	22	19	16
Chinese cabbage												
Prepare and enrich soil				5	2/29	26						
Sow in place						8	5	2/29	25			
Thin out, maintain						26	23	19	7/16	13		
Harvest									25	22	19	16
Head cabbage												
Prepare and enrich soil		9	8	5						13	9	
Sow in warm conditions	22	19										
Transplant in nursery			9	8	5					4		
Sow in nursery			18	14	2/12/29	26		29	7/16	13		
Plant, maintain				8	5	2/12/29	8/26	23	19	7/16	13	9
Harvest					12	8	5	2/29	25	22	19	16
Kale												
Prepare and enrich soil		9	8	5						13	9	
Sow in nursery				14	12	8						
Transplant in nursery, maintain					2/29	26	23					
Plant, maintain						26	23	19	7/16	13		
Harvest										22	19	16
Savoy cabbage												
Prepare and enrich soil		9	8	5						13	9	
Sow in nursery			18	15	12	8						
Transplant in nursery, maintain				5	2/29	26	23					
Plant, maintain					2/29	26	23	19	7.16	13		
Harvest	22	19	18						25	22	19	16

The cultivation of the vegetable is explained in the Calendar on the highlighted date.

Year-round salad leaves

- Sow and plant in the greenhouse, under cover or in the open depending on the season and the climate of your garden
- Sow with the ascending moon in Pisces ♓
- Plant, hoe and earth up with the descending moon in Cancer ♋ or Scorpio ♏

	Jan	Feb	Mar	Apr	May	Jun	Jul	Aug	Sep	Oct	Nov	Dec
Cress												
Sow	22	19	18	14	12	8	5	2/29	25	22	19	16
Sow			18	14	12	8						
Dandelion												
Sow	22	19	18	14	12	8	5	2/29	25	22	19	16
Pull out, plant			18	14	12	8						
Endive (chicory)												
Curly endive												
Sow			18	14	12	8	5					
Transplant, maintain				5/22	2/29	26	23	19	7/16	13	9	
Escarole												
Sow					12	8	5					
Transplant, plant, maintain						26	23	19	7/16	13		
Radicchio												
Sow					12	8	5					
Thin out, maintain						26	23	19	7/16	13		
Wild chicory												
Sow					12	8	5					
Thin out, maintain						26	23	19	7/16	13		
Lettuce												
Batavia												
Sow	22	19	18	14	12	8	5	2/29	25			
Transplant, plant, maintain		9	8	5	2/29	26	23	19	7/16	13	9	
'Cut and come again' lettuce												
Sow	22	19	18	14	12	8	5	2/29	25			
Transplant, plant, maintain		9	8	5	2/29	26	23	19	7/16	13	9	
Head lettuce												
Sow	22	19	18	14	12	8	5	2/29				
Transplant, plant, maintain		9	8	5	2/29	26	23	19	7/16			
Lamb's lettuce (mâche)												
Sow							5	2/29	25			
Romaine												
Sow		19	18	14	12	8	5	2/29				
Transplant, plant, maintain			8	5	2/29	26	23	19	7/16			
Winter lettuce												
Sow								2/29	25	22		
Transplant, plant, maintain	3/13	9	8	5	2/29			19	7/16	13	9	6/25
Purslane												
Sow	22	19	18	14	12	8	5	2/29				16
Rocket (arugula)												
Sow		19	18	14	12	8	5	2/29	25			

The cultivation of the vegetable is explained in the Calendar on the highlighted date.

Aromatic herbs

- Sow and plant in the greenhouse, under cover or in the open depending on the season and the climate of your garden
- Sow with the ascending moon in Pisces ♓
- Plant, divide and prune with the descending moon in Cancer ♋ or Scorpio ♏

		Jan	Feb	Mar	Apr	May	Jun	Jul	Aug	Sep	Oct	Nov	Dec
Annuals													
Basil	Sow in sheltered location			18	14								
	Plant				5	2/29							
Chervil	Sow in sheltered location	22	19								22		
	Sow in the sun			18	14					25			
	Sow in the shade					12	8	5	2/29				
	Thin out, remove flowers		9	8	5	2/29	26	23	19	7/16	13	9	
Coriander (cilantro)	Sow				14	12	8			25			
Dill	Sow				14	12	8						
Marjoram	Sow			18	14	12				25			
Parsley	Sow		19	18	14	12	8	5	2/29				
	Thin out, remove flowers			8	5	2/29	26	23	19	7/16			
Perennials													
Bay (laurel)	Plant, prune			8	5	2/29				7/16	13		
	Take cuttings								19	7/16	13		
Chive	Sow			18	14								
	Thin out, transplant				5	2/29							
	Plant, divide			8	5	2/29				7/16	13		
Lemon-balm	Sow					12	8						
	Plant, divide			8	5	2/29				7/16	13		
Mint	Sow			8	5	2/29							
	Turn down						26	23			13	9	
Oregano	Sow			18	14	12				25			
	Plant, divide			8	5	2/29				7/16	13		
Rosemary	Plant			8	5	2/29							
	Take cuttings				5	2/29			19	7/16			
Sage	Plant, prune			8	5	2/29							
	Make cuttings					2/29			19	7/16			
Savory	Plant			8	5	2/29				7/16			
	Take cuttings								19	7/16			
Sorrel	Sow		19	18	14	12	8						
	Plant, divide		9	8	5						13	9	
Tarragon	Plant, divide			8	5	2/29							
	Turn down, protect										13	9	
Thyme	Sow					12	8						
	Plant, divide			8	5	2/29				7/16	13		
	Prune												

The cultivation of the vegetable is explained in the Calendar on the highlighted date.

Root vegetables

- Sow and plant in the greenhouse, under cover or in the open depending on the season and the climate of your garden
- Sow with the ascendant Moon in Taurus ♉ or Capricorn ♑
- Do all other garden work with the descending moon in Virgo ♍

Crop	Activity	Jan	Feb	Mar	Apr	May	Jun	Jul	Aug	Sep	Oct	Nov	Dec
Beet(root)	→ Sow (soil at 10 °C/50 °F*)				18	8/16	4/12						
	→ Thin out, hoe				27	24	20	18	14	10	8		
	→ Harvest							18	14	10	8	4	
Carrot	→ Sow (soil at 10 °C/50 °F*)	17/26	14/23	13/22	18	8/16	4/12	1/10/28		2/21/29	1/18/27	15/23	
	→ Weed, thin		4	3/30	1/27	24	20	18	14	10	8	4	1/29
	→ Harvest				1/27	24	20	18	14	10	8	4	1/29
Celeriac	→ Sow (soil at 12 °C/53 °F*)		14/23	13/22	18	8/16							
	→ Transplant twice, plant			3/30	1/27	24	20						
	→ Harvest								14	10	8	4	
Chicory/witloof/ Belgian endive)	→ Sow (soil at 14 °C/57 °F*)					8/16	4/12						
	→ Thin, weed					24	20	18	14	10	8		
	→ Pull out, then replant**										8		
Chinese artichoke	→ Plant		4	3/30	1/27								
	→ Hoe, weed			3/30	1/27	24	20	18	14	10	8		
	→ Transplant	7	4	3/30							8	4	1/29
Garlic	→ Plant, hoe	7	4	3.30							8	4	1/29
	→ Harvest						24	20	18	14			
Leek	→ Sow (soil at 10 °C/50 °F*)	17/26	14/23	13/22	18	8/16			6/25	2/21/29			
	→ Thin, plant, hoe		4	3/30	1/27	24	20	18	14	10	8	4	
	→ Harvest	7	4	3/30	1/27	24	20	18	14	10	8	4	1/29
Onion (coloured)	→ Sow (soil at 10 °C/50 °F*)		14/23	13/22	18				25	2			
	→ Thin, plant, hoe				1/27	24	20	18	14	10	8	4	
	→ Harvest					24	20	18	14				
Onion (white)	→ Sow (soil at 10 °C/50 °F*)	17/26	14/23	13/22	18				25	2			
	→ Thin, plant, hoe			3/30	1/27	24	20	18		10	8	4	
	→ Harvest					24	20	18					
Potato	→ Plant		4	3/30	1/27								
	→ Mound with soil, hoe, harvest			3/30	1/27	24	20	18	14	10			
Radish	→ Sow (soil at 12 °C/53 °F*)	17/26	14/23	13/22	18	8/16	4/12	1/10/28	6/25	2/21/29	1/18/27	15/23	11/20
	→ Thin, harvest	7	4	3/30	1/27	24	20	18	14	10	8	4	1/29
Salsify	→ Sow (soil at 15 °C/59 °F*)			13/22	18	8/16			6/25				
	→ Thin, hoe, pinch				1/27	24	20	18	14	10	8		
	→ Harvest	7	4								8	4	1/29
Shallot	→ Plant, weed	7	4	3/30	1/27	24	20	18			8	4	1/29
	→ Harvest						20	18	14				
Turnip	→ Sow (soil at 15 °C/59 °F*)	1/17/26	14/23	13/22	18	8/16	4/12	1/10/28	6/25				
	→ Thin, hoe, water		4	3/30	1/27	24	20	18	14	10	8		
	→ Transplant				1/27	24	20	18	14	10	8	4	

The cultivation of the vegetable is explained in the Calendar on the highlighted date.
*Ideal soil temperature for good germination.
** See more in leafy vegetables (p. 107).

Fruit vegetables

- Sow and plant in the greenhouse, under cover or in the open depending on the season and the climate of your garden
- Sow with the ascendant moon in Aries ♈ or Sagittarius ♐
- Do all other work with the descending moon in Leo ♌

Aubergine

	Jan	Feb	Mar	Apr	May	Jun	Jul	Aug	Sep	Oct	Nov	Dec
→ Sow (in warm location at 20 °C/68 °F*)	16	12	12									
→ Transplant, plant, prune		1	2/28	24	22/31	18	15	12	9			
→ Harvest							26	22/31	19/28	16		

Beans

	Jan	Feb	Mar	Apr	May	Jun	Jul	Aug	Sep	Oct	Nov	Dec
→ Sow (soil at 10–12 °C/50–53 °F*)					5	29	26					
→ Hoe, earth up					22/31	18	15	12	9			
→ Harvest							26	22/31	19/28	16		

Broad beans (fava)

	Jan	Feb	Mar	Apr	May	Jun	Jul	Aug	Sep	Oct	Nov	Dec
→ Sow (soil at 8–10 °C/46–50 °F*)	16	12	12							16	12	19
→ Hoe, earth up, cut tops	5	1	2/28	24	22/31	18	15				2/29	26
→ Transplant				8	5	29	26	22				

Pepper (chilli and sweet)

	Jan	Feb	Mar	Apr	May	Jun	Jul	Aug	Sep	Oct	Nov	Dec
→ Sow (in warm location at 20 °C/68 °F*)	16	12	12									
→ Transplant, plant, cut back		1	2/28	24	22/31	18	15	12	9			
→ Harvest							26	22/31	19/28	16		

Cucumber

	Jan	Feb	Mar	Apr	May	Jun	Jul	Aug	Sep	Oct	Nov	Dec
→ Sow (soil at 18 °C/64 °F*)			12	8	5	29						
→ Thin, plant, prune			28	24	22/31	18	15	12	9			
→ Harvest						29	26	22/31	19/28	16		

Melon

	Jan	Feb	Mar	Apr	May	Jun	Jul	Aug	Sep	Oct	Nov	Dec
→ Sow (soil at 20 °C/68 °F*)		12	8	5								
→ Transplant, plant, cut back				24	22/31	18	15	12				
→ Harvest							26	22/31	19/28			

Peas (round)

	Jan	Feb	Mar	Apr	May	Jun	Jul	Aug	Sep	Oct	Nov	Dec
→ Sow (soil at 10 °C/50 °F*)	16	12	12	8	5					16	12	19
→ Hoe, earth up	5	1	2/28	24	22/31	18	15				2/29	26
→ Harvest				8	5	29	26					

Squash and courgette (zucchini)

	Jan	Feb	Mar	Apr	May	Jun	Jul	Aug	Sep	Oct	Nov	Dec
→ Sow (soil at 14 °C/57 °F*)			12	8	5	29						
→ Thin, plant, prune			28	24	22/31	18	15	12	9			
→ Harvest						29	26	22/31	19/28	16		

Strawberry

	Jan	Feb	Mar	Apr	May	Jun	Jul	Aug	Sep	Oct	Nov	Dec
→ Plant			2/28	24				12	9	6		
→ Harvest					5	29	26	22/31	19/28	16		

Tomato

	Jan	Feb	Mar	Apr	May	Jun	Jul	Aug	Sep	Oct	Nov	Dec
→ Sow (soil at 16–20 °C/60–68 °F*)		12	12	8								
→ Transplant, plant, prune			2/28	24	22/31	18	15	12	9			
→ Harvest						29	26	22/31	19/28	16		

The cultivation of the vegetable is explained in the Calendar on the highlighted date.
*Ideal soil temperature for good germination.

In the Orchard

- Plant, prune, clear and make cuttings with the descending moon in Leo ♌
- Graft in the ascending moon in Aries ♈ or Sagittarius ♐

		Jan	Feb	Mar	Apr	May	Jun	Jul	Aug	Sep	Oct	Nov	Dec
Fruit Trees and Shrubs													
Plant	→ Prepare planting holes, fertilise	5	1	2/28	24				12	9	6	2/29	26
	→ Put fruit trees and small-fruit shrubs in place	5	1	2/28	24					9	6	2/29	26
Prune	→ Crops with pips: apple, pear trees and grapes	5	1	2/28								2/29	26
	→ Apricot and peach trees		1	2/28									
	→ Small fruit bushes	5	1	2/28			18	15	12				
	→ When green, prune apples, pears, grapes						18	15	12				
	→ After the harvest, prune apricot and peach trees								12	9			
Treat the trees	→ With white oil in winter	5	1									2/29	26
	→ With fungicide twice a year: before budding and when leaves fall		1	2/28							6	2/29	
Thin	→ Apples, pears, peaches						31	18					
Propagate	→ Make cuttings of small fruit shrubs	5	1	2/28								2/29	26
	→ Graft fruit-bearing trees			12	8		11/29	26	22				
	→ Layer grapes and kiwi			2/28	24	22/31	18						
Olive Trees													
	→ Plant			2/28									
	→ Prune, treat		1	2/28							6	2/29	
	→ Fertilise				24	22.31		15			6		

Wood for Timber and Heating

	Jan	Feb	Mar	Apr	May	Jun	Jul	Aug	Sep	Oct	Nov	Dec
Cut down large trees, cut up trunks, split logs	**In descending Moon:** January 2–15, January 30–February 11, February 26–March 10, March 25–31.									**In descending Moon:** October 3–15, October 30–November 11, November 26–December 8, December 24–31.		

The cultivation of the vegetable is explained in the Calendar on the highlighted date.

In the Ornamental Garden

- Thin, transplant, cut back, make cuttings, layer, divide and fertilise with the descending Moon in Gemini ♊ or Libra ♎
- Sow and graft with the ascending moon in Aquarius ♒

		Jan	Feb	Mar	Apr	May	Jun	Jul	Aug	Sep	Oct	Nov	Dec
Annual flowers													
nasturtium, petunia, zinnia, clarkia...	Sow	20	16	15	12	9	6		26	23	20		13
	Thin, transplant, plant	2/11	7/26	6/25	3/30	1/19/27	15/24	21			3/11/30	7	
Biennial flowers													
wallflower, forget-me-not, daisy, pansy...	Sow					9	6	3/30	26				
	Thin, transplant						15/24	21	9/17	14	3/11/30	7	
Perennial flowers													
oriental poppy, hollyhock, columbine, aster, peony...	Sow			15		9	6	3/30	26	23	20	16	
	Thin, transplant				3/30		15/24	21	9/17	14	3/11/30	7	
	Divide			6/25	3/30				17	14	3/11/30	7	
Perennial bulbs													
Spring flowering													
snowdrop, crocus, anemone, narcissus, hyacinth, tulip...	Plant		7/26	6/25						14	3/11/30	7	
	Divide		7/26	6/25			1/19/27	15/24					
Summer flowering													
madonna lily	Plant							21	9/17	14			
other lilies	Plant		7/26	6/25						14	3/11/30	7	
canna, dahlia, gladiola...	Plant	2/11	7/26	6/25	3/30	1/19/27							
	Pinch back					1/19/27	15/24	21	9/17	14			
	Pull out										3/11/30	7	
Perennial rhizomes													
iris	Plant, divide							21	9/17	14			
Perennial vines													
clematis, honeysuckle, wisteria...	Plant	2/11	7/26	6/25	3/30					14	3/11/30	7	4
	Prune		7/26	6/25								7	4
	Layer				3/30	1/19/27	15/24	21	9/17				
Roses													
	Plant	2/11	7/26	6/25								7	4
	Prune suckers		7/26	6/25							7		
	Remove dead leaves							21	9/17				
	Deadhead flowers					1/19/27	15/24	21	9/17	14	3/11/30		
	Make cuttings								9/17	14			
	Fertilise		7/26	6/25								7	4
	T-bud (shield graft)							30	26	23			
Spring or summer-blooming shrubs													
magnolia, forsythia, lilac, rhododendron, hydrangea...	Plant	2/11	7/26	6/25	3/30					14	3/11/30	7	4
	Prune			6/25	3/30	1/19/27	15/24						
	Take cuttings			6/25	3/30	1/19/27	15/24	21	9/17	14			
	Fertilise		7/26	6/25								7	4
	Graft		16	15			6	3/30	26	23			

The cultivation of the vegetable is explained in the Calendar on the highlighted date.

Trees, shrubs, leafy vines

- Plant, cut back, prune, cut stakes, clear and plant cuttings with the descending Moon in Cancer ♋ or Scorpio ♏.

		Jan	Feb	Mar	Apr	May	Jun	Jul	Aug	Sep	Oct	Nov	Dec
Conifers													
cedar, cypress, thuja, pine, fir, spruce...	Plant			8	5					7/16	13		
	Prune			8	5				19	7/16			
	Take cuttings			8					19	7/16			
Deciduous trees and shrubs													
birch, hornbeam, maple, beech, poplar, plane tree, prunus, willow...	Plant	3/13	9	8	5						13	9	6/25
	Prune		9	8	5		26	23	19	7/16			
	Thin	3/13	9									9	6/25
	Remove stakes	3/13	9									9	6/25
	Clear brush						26	23	19				
	Take cuttings		9	8			26	23	19	7/16	13	9	
Evergreen shrubs and bushes													
boxwood, spindle tree, holly, bay (laurel)...	Plant		9	8	5					7/16	13	9	
	Prune		9	8	5	2/29	26		19	7/16			
	Take cuttings		9	8						7/16			
Vines													
ivy, Virginia creeper...	Plant		9	8	5					7/16	13	9	6/25
	Prune			8		2/29	26	23	19				
	Take cuttings			8	5						13	9	

The lawn

- Sow with the ascending moon in Pisces ♓
- Do all other tasks with the descending Moon in Cancer ♋ or Scorpio ♏.

		Jan	Feb	Mar	Apr	May	Jun	Jul	Aug	Sep	Oct	Nov	Dec
Bare spots	→ Rake the soil, spread mulch, roll			8	5	2			19	7/16			
	→ Sow, roll, water				14	12				25			
For new lawns	→ Prepare the soil		9	8	5			23	19	7/16			
	→ Spread compost		9	8	5				19	7/16			
	→ Level, rake, roll		9	8	5				19	7/16			
	→ Sow				14	12				25			
Yearly maintenance	→ Rake			8	5								
	→ Weed			8	5	2/29				7/16	13		
	→ Fertilise			8	5								6/25
	→ Mow, water			8	5	2/29	26	23	19	7/16	13		

In winter, don't walk on your lawn if it is frozen or under snow as you will damage the grass.

The cultivation of the vegetable is explained in the Calendar on the highlighted date.

Index

Other books you might find useful

The original lunar sowing and planting calendar, now in its 56th year. Especially good if you're keen on the astronomy behind the practice.

Explains what weeds can tell us about the health of our soil. A fascinating little book.

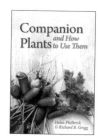

The definitive guide to companion planting (see pp. 27–29) to get the best from your plants.

An illustrated, non-jargon introduction to the world of biodynamic planting and growing.

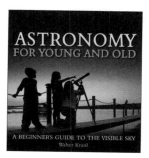

If you'd like to find out more about astronomy, this book is a readable introduction. Great for kids too!

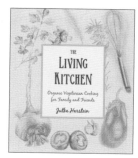

A cookbook which harnesses all the goodness and deliciousness of your garden produce. Easy-to-follow recipes full of life forces.

Get your children and grandchildren gardening! Fun and practical activities to do in the garden every month of the year.

Race handmade boats, build an insect hotel and create wildflower Easter eggs, all while learning about the natural world – whatever the weather.

Create pine-cone gnomes, build nesting boxes for garden birds, and craft festive angels. More great seasonal nature activities for your children and grandchildren.

Why not try the
Maria Thun Biodynamic Calendar app?

Try it for free!

 Automatically adjusts to your time-zone –
no need for manual calculations

 Ideal for farmers and gardeners worldwide

 Choose your language – English, German or Dutch

Based on the *Maria Thun Biodynamic Calendar*,
the app is a quick, easy way to look up the key sowing
and planting information by date or type of action
(harvesting, sowing, grafting, etc) – and it's always in
your pocket on your phone.

For iPhone and iPad.